Moses Maimonides: A Very Short Introduction

VERY SHORT INTRODUCTIONS are for anyone wanting a stimulating and accessible way into a new subject. They are written by experts, and have been translated into more than 45 different languages.

The series began in 1995, and now covers a wide variety of topics in every discipline. The VSI library currently contains over 750 volumes—a Very Short Introduction to everything from Psychology and Philosophy of Science to American History and Relativity—and continues to grow in every subject area.

Very Short Introductions available now:

ABOLITIONISM Richard S. Newman
THE ABRAHAMIC RELIGIONS
    Charles L. Cohen
ACCOUNTING Christopher Nobes
ADDICTION Keith Humphreys
ADOLESCENCE Peter K. Smith
THEODOR W. ADORNO
    Andrew Bowie
ADVERTISING Winston Fletcher
AERIAL WARFARE Frank Ledwidge
AESTHETICS Bence Nanay
AFRICAN AMERICAN HISTORY
    Jonathan Scott Holloway
AFRICAN AMERICAN RELIGION
    Eddie S. Glaude Jr.
AFRICAN HISTORY John Parker and
    Richard Rathbone
AFRICAN POLITICS Ian Taylor
AFRICAN RELIGIONS
    Jacob K. Olupona
AGEING Nancy A. Pachana
AGNOSTICISM Robin Le Poidevin
AGRICULTURE Paul Brassley and
    Richard Soffe
ALEXANDER THE GREAT
    Hugh Bowden
ALGEBRA Peter M. Higgins
AMERICAN BUSINESS HISTORY
    Walter A. Friedman
AMERICAN CULTURAL HISTORY
    Eric Avila
AMERICAN FOREIGN RELATIONS
    Andrew Preston
AMERICAN HISTORY Paul S. Boyer

AMERICAN IMMIGRATION
    David A. Gerber
AMERICAN INTELLECTUAL
    HISTORY
    Jennifer Ratner-Rosenhagen
THE AMERICAN JUDICIAL SYSTEM
    Charles L. Zelden
AMERICAN LEGAL HISTORY
    G. Edward White
AMERICAN MILITARY HISTORY
    Joseph T. Glatthaar
AMERICAN NAVAL HISTORY
    Craig L. Symonds
AMERICAN POETRY David Caplan
AMERICAN POLITICAL HISTORY
    Donald Critchlow
AMERICAN POLITICAL PARTIES
    AND ELECTIONS L. Sandy Maisel
AMERICAN POLITICS
    Richard M. Valelly
THE AMERICAN PRESIDENCY
    Charles O. Jones
THE AMERICAN REVOLUTION
    Robert J. Allison
AMERICAN SLAVERY
    Heather Andrea Williams
THE AMERICAN SOUTH
    Charles Reagan Wilson
THE AMERICAN WEST
    Stephen Aron
AMERICAN WOMEN'S HISTORY
    Susan Ware
AMPHIBIANS T. S. Kemp
ANAESTHESIA Aidan O'Donnell

ANALYTIC PHILOSOPHY
Michael Beaney
ANARCHISM Alex Prichard
ANCIENT ASSYRIA Karen Radner
ANCIENT EGYPT Ian Shaw
ANCIENT EGYPTIAN ART AND
ARCHITECTURE Christina Riggs
ANCIENT GREECE Paul Cartledge
ANCIENT GREEK AND ROMAN
SCIENCE Liba Taub
THE ANCIENT NEAR EAST
Amanda H. Podany
ANCIENT PHILOSOPHY Julia Annas
ANCIENT WARFARE
Harry Sidebottom
ANGELS David Albert Jones
ANGLICANISM Mark Chapman
THE ANGLO-SAXON AGE John Blair
ANIMAL BEHAVIOUR
Tristram D. Wyatt
THE ANIMAL KINGDOM
Peter Holland
ANIMAL RIGHTS David DeGrazia
ANSELM Thomas Williams
THE ANTARCTIC Klaus Dodds
ANTHROPOCENE Erle C. Ellis
ANTISEMITISM Steven Beller
ANXIETY Daniel Freeman and
Jason Freeman
THE APOCRYPHAL GOSPELS
Paul Foster
APPLIED MATHEMATICS
Alain Goriely
THOMAS AQUINAS Fergus Kerr
ARBITRATION Thomas Schultz and
Thomas Grant
ARCHAEOLOGY Paul Bahn
ARCHITECTURE Andrew Ballantyne
THE ARCTIC Klaus Dodds and
Jamie Woodward
HANNAH ARENDT Dana Villa
ARISTOCRACY William Doyle
ARISTOTLE Jonathan Barnes
ART HISTORY Dana Arnold
ART THEORY Cynthia Freeland
ARTIFICIAL INTELLIGENCE
Margaret A. Boden
ASIAN AMERICAN HISTORY
Madeline Y. Hsu
ASTROBIOLOGY David C. Catling

ASTROPHYSICS James Binney
ATHEISM Julian Baggini
THE ATMOSPHERE Paul I. Palmer
AUGUSTINE Henry Chadwick
JANE AUSTEN Tom Keymer
AUSTRALIA Kenneth Morgan
AUTHORITARIANISM James Loxton
AUTISM Uta Frith
AUTOBIOGRAPHY Laura Marcus
THE AVANT GARDE David Cottington
THE AZTECS Davíd Carrasco
BABYLONIA Trevor Bryce
BACTERIA Sebastian G. B. Amyes
BANKING John Goddard and
John O. S. Wilson
BARTHES Jonathan Culler
THE BEATS David Sterritt
BEAUTY Roger Scruton
LUDWIG VAN BEETHOVEN
Mark Evan Bonds
BEHAVIOURAL ECONOMICS
Michelle Baddeley
BESTSELLERS John Sutherland
THE BIBLE John Riches
BIBLICAL ARCHAEOLOGY
Eric H. Cline
BIG DATA Dawn E. Holmes
BIOCHEMISTRY Mark Lorch
BIODIVERSITY CONSERVATION
David Macdonald
BIOGEOGRAPHY Mark V. Lomolino
BIOGRAPHY Hermione Lee
BIOMETRICS Michael Fairhurst
ELIZABETH BISHOP
Jonathan F. S. Post
BLACK HOLES Katherine Blundell
BLASPHEMY Yvonne Sherwood
BLOOD Chris Cooper
THE BLUES Elijah Wald
THE BODY Chris Shilling
THE BOHEMIANS David Weir
NIELS BOHR J. L. Heilbron
THE BOOK OF COMMON PRAYER
Brian Cummings
THE BOOK OF MORMON
Terryl Givens
BORDERS Alexander C. Diener and
Joshua Hagen
JORGE LUIS BORGES Ilan Stavans
THE BRAIN Michael O'Shea

BRANDING Robert Jones
THE BRICS Andrew F. Cooper
BRITISH ARCHITECTURE
Dana Arnold
BRITISH CINEMA Charles Barr
THE BRITISH CONSTITUTION
Martin Loughlin
THE BRITISH EMPIRE Ashley Jackson
BRITISH POLITICS Tony Wright
BUDDHA Michael Carrithers
BUDDHISM Damien Keown
BUDDHIST ETHICS Damien Keown
BYZANTIUM Peter Sarris
CALVINISM Jon Balserak
ALBERT CAMUS Oliver Gloag
CANADA Donald Wright
CANCER Nicholas James
CAPITALISM James Fulcher
CATHOLICISM Gerald O'Collins
THE CATHOLIC REFORMATION
James E. Kelly
CAUSATION Stephen Mumford and
Rani Lill Anjum
THE CELL Terence Allen and
Graham Cowling
THE CELTS Barry Cunliffe
CHAOS Leonard Smith
GEOFFREY CHAUCER David Wallace
CHEMISTRY Peter Atkins
CHILD PSYCHOLOGY Usha Goswami
CHILDREN'S LITERATURE
Kimberley Reynolds
CHINESE LITERATURE Sabina Knight
CHOICE THEORY Michael Allingham
CHRISTIAN ART Beth Williamson
CHRISTIAN ETHICS D. Stephen Long
CHRISTIANITY Linda Woodhead
CIRCADIAN RHYTHMS
Russell Foster and Leon Kreitzman
CITIZENSHIP Richard Bellamy
CITY PLANNING Carl Abbott
CIVIL ENGINEERING
David Muir Wood
THE CIVIL RIGHTS MOVEMENT
Thomas C. Holt
CIVIL WARS Monica Duffy Toft
CLASSICAL LITERATURE
William Allan
CLASSICAL MYTHOLOGY
Helen Morales

CLASSICS Mary Beard and
John Henderson
CLAUSEWITZ Michael Howard
CLIMATE Mark Maslin
CLIMATE CHANGE Mark Maslin
CLINICAL PSYCHOLOGY
Susan Llewelyn and
Katie Aafjes-van Doorn
COGNITIVE BEHAVIOURAL
THERAPY Freda McManus
COGNITIVE NEUROSCIENCE
Richard Passingham
THE COLD WAR Robert J. McMahon
COLONIAL AMERICA Alan Taylor
COLONIAL LATIN AMERICAN
LITERATURE Rolena Adorno
COMBINATORICS Robin Wilson
COMEDY Matthew Bevis
COMMUNISM Leslie Holmes
COMPARATIVE LAW Sabrina Ragone
and Guido Smorto
COMPARATIVE LITERATURE
Ben Hutchinson
COMPETITION AND
ANTITRUST LAW Ariel Ezrachi
COMPLEXITY John H. Holland
THE COMPUTER Darrel Ince
COMPUTER SCIENCE
Subrata Dasgupta
CONCENTRATION CAMPS
Dan Stone
CONDENSED MATTER PHYSICS
Ross H. McKenzie
CONFUCIANISM Daniel K. Gardner
THE CONQUISTADORS
Matthew Restall and
Felipe Fernández-Armesto
CONSCIENCE Paul Strohm
CONSCIOUSNESS Susan Blackmore
CONTEMPORARY ART
Julian Stallabrass
CONTEMPORARY FICTION
Robert Eaglestone
CONTINENTAL PHILOSOPHY
Simon Critchley
COPERNICUS Owen Gingerich
CORAL REEFS Charles Sheppard
CORPORATE SOCIAL
RESPONSIBILITY Jeremy Moon
CORRUPTION Leslie Holmes

COSMOLOGY Peter Coles
COUNTRY MUSIC Richard Carlin
CREATIVITY Vlad Glăveanu
CRIME FICTION Richard Bradford
CRIMINAL JUSTICE Julian V. Roberts
CRIMINOLOGY Tim Newburn
CRITICAL THEORY
Stephen Eric Bronner
THE CRUSADES Christopher Tyerman
CRYPTOGRAPHY Sean Murphy and
Rachel Player
CRYSTALLOGRAPHY A. M. Glazer
THE CULTURAL REVOLUTION
Richard Curt Kraus
DADA AND SURREALISM
David Hopkins
DANTE Peter Hainsworth and
David Robey
DARWIN Jonathan Howard
THE DEAD SEA SCROLLS
Timothy H. Lim
DECADENCE David Weir
DECOLONIZATION Dane Kennedy
DEMENTIA Kathleen Taylor
DEMOCRACY Naomi Zack
DEMOGRAPHY Sarah Harper
DEPRESSION Jan Scott and
Mary Jane Tacchi
DERRIDA Simon Glendinning
DESCARTES Tom Sorell
DESERTS Nick Middleton
DESIGN John Heskett
DEVELOPMENT Ian Goldin
DEVELOPMENTAL BIOLOGY
Lewis Wolpert
THE DEVIL Darren Oldridge
DIASPORA Kevin Kenny
CHARLES DICKENS Jenny Hartley
DICTIONARIES Lynda Mugglestone
DINOSAURS David Norman
DIPLOMATIC HISTORY
Joseph M. Siracusa
DOCUMENTARY FILM
Patricia Aufderheide
DOSTOEVSKY Deborah Martinsen
DREAMING J. Allan Hobson
DRUGS Les Iversen
DRUIDS Barry Cunliffe
DYNASTY Jeroen Duindam
DYSLEXIA Margaret J. Snowling

EARLY MUSIC Thomas Forrest Kelly
THE EARTH Martin Redfern
EARTH SYSTEM SCIENCE Tim Lenton
ECOLOGY Jaboury Ghazoul
ECONOMICS Partha Dasgupta
EDUCATION Gary Thomas
EGYPTIAN MYTH Geraldine Pinch
EIGHTEENTH-CENTURY BRITAIN
Paul Langford
ELECTIONS L. Sandy Maisel and
Jennifer A. Yoder
THE ELEMENTS Philip Ball
GEORGE ELIOT Juliette Atkinson
EMOTION Dylan Evans
EMPIRE Stephen Howe
EMPLOYMENT LAW David Cabrelli
ENERGY SYSTEMS Nick Jenkins
ENGELS Terrell Carver
ENGINEERING David Blockley
THE ENGLISH LANGUAGE
Simon Horobin
ENGLISH LITERATURE
Jonathan Bate
THE ENLIGHTENMENT
John Robertson
ENTREPRENEURSHIP Paul Westhead
and Mike Wright
ENVIRONMENTAL ECONOMICS
Stephen Smith
ENVIRONMENTAL ETHICS
Robin Attfield
ENVIRONMENTAL LAW
Elizabeth Fisher
ENVIRONMENTAL POLITICS
Andrew Dobson
ENZYMES Paul Engel
THE EPIC Anthony Welch
EPICUREANISM Catherine Wilson
EPIDEMIOLOGY Rodolfo Saracci
ETHICS Simon Blackburn
ETHNOMUSICOLOGY Timothy Rice
THE ETRUSCANS Christopher Smith
EUGENICS Philippa Levine
THE EUROPEAN UNION
Simon Usherwood and John Pinder
EUROPEAN UNION LAW
Anthony Arnull
EVANGELICALISM
John G. Stackhouse Jr.
EVIL Luke Russell

EVOLUTION Brian and
    Deborah Charlesworth
EXISTENTIALISM Thomas Flynn
EXPLORATION Stewart A. Weaver
EXTINCTION Paul B. Wignall
THE EYE Michael Land
FAIRY TALE Marina Warner
FAITH Roger Trigg
FAMILY LAW Jonathan Herring
MICHAEL FARADAY
    Frank A. J. L. James
FASCISM Kevin Passmore
FASHION Rebecca Arnold
FEDERALISM Mark J. Rozell and
    Clyde Wilcox
FEMINISM Margaret Walters
FEMINIST PHILOSOPHY
    Katharine Jenkins
FILM Michael Wood
FILM MUSIC Kathryn Kalinak
FILM NOIR James Naremore
FIRE Andrew C. Scott
THE FIRST WORLD WAR
    Michael Howard
FLUID MECHANICS Eric Lauga
FOLK MUSIC Mark Slobin
FOOD John Krebs
FORENSIC PSYCHOLOGY
    David Canter
FORENSIC SCIENCE Jim Fraser
FORESTS Jaboury Ghazoul
FOSSILS Keith Thomson
FOUCAULT Gary Gutting
THE FOUNDING FATHERS
    R. B. Bernstein
FRACTALS Kenneth Falconer
FREE SPEECH Nigel Warburton
FREE WILL Thomas Pink
FREEMASONRY Andreas Önnerfors
FRENCH CINEMA Dudley Andrew
FRENCH LITERATURE John D. Lyons
FRENCH PHILOSOPHY
    Stephen Gaukroger and Knox Peden
THE FRENCH REVOLUTION
    William Doyle
FREUD Anthony Storr
FUNDAMENTALISM Malise Ruthven
FUNGI Nicholas P. Money
THE FUTURE Jennifer M. Gidley
FUTURSM Ara Merjian

GALAXIES John Gribbin
GALILEO Stillman Drake
GAME THEORY Ken Binmore
GANDHI Bhikhu Parekh
GARDEN HISTORY Gordon Campbell
GENDER HISTORY Antoinette Burton
GENES Jonathan Slack
GENIUS Andrew Robinson
GENOMICS John Archibald
GEOGRAPHY John Matthews and
    David Herbert
GEOLOGY Jan Zalasiewicz
GEOMETRY Maciej Dunajski
GEOPHYSICAL AND
    CLIMATE HAZARDS Bill McGuire
GEOPHYSICS William Lowrie
GEOPOLITICS Klaus Dodds
GERMAN LITERATURE Nicholas Boyle
GERMAN PHILOSOPHY
    Andrew Bowie
THE GHETTO Bryan Cheyette
GLACIATION David J. A. Evans
GLOBAL ECONOMIC HISTORY
    Robert C. Allen
GLOBAL ISLAM Nile Green
GLOBALIZATION Manfred B. Steger
GOD John Bowker
GÖDEL'S THEOREM A. W. Moore
GOETHE Ritchie Robertson
THE GOTHIC Nick Groom
GOVERNANCE Mark Bevir
GRAVITY Timothy Clifton
THE GREAT DEPRESSION AND
    THE NEW DEAL Eric Rauchway
THE GULAG Alan Barenberg
HABEAS CORPUS Amanda L. Tyler
HABERMAS James Gordon Finlayson
THE HABSBURG EMPIRE
    Martyn Rady
HAPPINESS Daniel M. Haybron
THE HARLEM RENAISSANCE
    Cheryl A. Wall
THE HEBREW BIBLE AS
    LITERATURE Tod Linafelt
HEGEL Peter Singer
HEIDEGGER Michael Inwood
THE HELLENISTIC AGE
    Peter Thonemann
HEREDITY John Waller
HERMENEUTICS Jens Zimmermann

HERODOTUS Jennifer T. Roberts
HIEROGLYPHS Penelope Wilson
HINDUISM Kim Knott
HISTORY John H. Arnold
THE HISTORY OF ASTRONOMY
    Michael Hoskin
THE HISTORY OF CHEMISTRY
    William H. Brock
THE HISTORY OF CHILDHOOD
    James Marten
THE HISTORY OF CINEMA
    Geoffrey Nowell-Smith
THE HISTORY OF COMPUTING
    Doron Swade
THE HISTORY OF EMOTIONS
    Thomas Dixon
THE HISTORY OF LIFE
    Michael Benton
THE HISTORY OF MATHEMATICS
    Jacqueline Stedall
THE HISTORY OF MEDICINE
    William Bynum
THE HISTORY OF PHYSICS
    J. L. Heilbron
THE HISTORY OF POLITICAL
    THOUGHT Richard Whatmore
THE HISTORY OF TIME
    Leofranc Holford-Strevens
HIV AND AIDS Alan Whiteside
HOBBES Richard Tuck
HOLLYWOOD Peter Decherney
THE HOLY ROMAN EMPIRE
    Joachim Whaley
HOME Michael Allen Fox
HOMER Barbara Graziosi
HORACE Llewelyn Morgan
HORMONES Martin Luck
HORROR Darryl Jones
HUMAN ANATOMY Leslie Klenerman
HUMAN EVOLUTION Bernard Wood
HUMAN PHYSIOLOGY
    Jamie A. Davies
HUMAN RESOURCE
    MANAGEMENT Adrian Wilkinson
HUMAN RIGHTS Andrew Clapham
HUMANISM Stephen Law
HUME James A. Harris
HUMOUR Noël Carroll
IBN SĪNĀ (AVICENNA)
    Peter Adamson

THE ICE AGE Jamie Woodward
IDENTITY Florian Coulmas
IDEOLOGY Michael Freeden
IMAGINATION
    Jennifer Gosetti-Ferencei
THE IMMUNE SYSTEM
    Paul Klenerman
INDIAN CINEMA
    Ashish Rajadhyaksha
INDIAN PHILOSOPHY Sue Hamilton
THE INDUSTRIAL REVOLUTION
    Robert C. Allen
INFECTIOUS DISEASE Marta L. Wayne
    and Benjamin M. Bolker
INFINITY Ian Stewart
INFORMATION Luciano Floridi
INNOVATION Mark Dodgson and
    David Gann
INTELLECTUAL PROPERTY
    Siva Vaidhyanathan
INTELLIGENCE Ian J. Deary
INTERNATIONAL LAW
    Vaughan Lowe
INTERNATIONAL MIGRATION
    Khalid Koser
INTERNATIONAL RELATIONS
    Christian Reus-Smit
INTERNATIONAL SECURITY
    Christopher S. Browning
INSECTS Simon Leather
INVASIVE SPECIES Julie Lockwood and
    Dustin Welbourne
IRAN Ali M. Ansari
ISLAM Malise Ruthven
ISLAMIC HISTORY Adam Silverstein
ISLAMIC LAW Mashood A. Baderin
ISOTOPES Rob Ellam
ITALIAN LITERATURE
    Peter Hainsworth and David Robey
HENRY JAMES Susan L. Mizruchi
JAPANESE LITERATURE Alan Tansman
JESUS Richard Bauckham
JEWISH HISTORY David N. Myers
JEWISH LITERATURE Ilan Stavans
JOURNALISM Ian Hargreaves
JAMES JOYCE Colin MacCabe
JUDAISM Norman Solomon
JUNG Anthony Stevens
THE JURY Renée Lettow Lerner
KABBALAH Joseph Dan

KAFKA Ritchie Robertson
KANT Roger Scruton
KEYNES Robert Skidelsky
KIERKEGAARD Patrick Gardiner
KNOWLEDGE Jennifer Nagel
THE KORAN Michael Cook
KOREA Michael J. Seth
LAKES Warwick F. Vincent
LANDSCAPE ARCHITECTURE
    Ian H. Thompson
LANDSCAPES AND
    GEOMORPHOLOGY
    Andrew Goudie and Heather Viles
LANGUAGES Stephen R. Anderson
LATE ANTIQUITY Gillian Clark
LAW Raymond Wacks
THE LAWS OF THERMODYNAMICS
    Peter Atkins
LEADERSHIP Keith Grint
LEARNING Mark Haselgrove
LEIBNIZ Maria Rosa Antognazza
C. S. LEWIS James Como
LIBERALISM Michael Freeden
LIGHT Ian Walmsley
LINCOLN Allen C. Guelzo
LINGUISTICS Peter Matthews
LITERARY THEORY Jonathan Culler
LOCKE John Dunn
LOGIC Graham Priest
LOVE Ronald de Sousa
MARTIN LUTHER Scott H. Hendrix
MACHIAVELLI Quentin Skinner
MADNESS Andrew Scull
MAGIC Owen Davies
MAGNA CARTA Nicholas Vincent
MAGNETISM Stephen Blundell
MOSES MAIMONIDES Ross Brann
MALTHUS Donald Winch
MAMMALS T. S. Kemp
MANAGEMENT John Hendry
NELSON MANDELA Elleke Boehmer
MAO Delia Davin
MARINE BIOLOGY
    Philip V. Mladenov
MARKETING
    Kenneth Le Meunier-FitzHugh
THE MARQUIS DE SADE John Phillips
MARTYRDOM Jolyon Mitchell
MARX Peter Singer
MATERIALS Christopher Hall

MATHEMATICAL ANALYSIS
    Richard Earl
MATHEMATICAL FINANCE
    Mark H. A. Davis
MATHEMATICS Timothy Gowers
MATTER Geoff Cottrell
THE MAYA Matthew Restall and
    Amara Solari
MEANING Emma Borg and
    Sarah A. Fisher
THE MEANING OF LIFE
    Terry Eagleton
MEASUREMENT David Hand
MEDICAL ETHICS Michael Dunn and
    Tony Hope
MEDICAL LAW Charles Foster
MEDIEVAL BRITAIN John Gillingham
    and Ralph A. Griffiths
MEDIEVAL LITERATURE
    Elaine Treharne
MEDIEVAL PHILOSOPHY
    John Marenbon
MEMORY Jonathan K. Foster
METAPHYSICS Stephen Mumford
METHODISM William J. Abraham
THE MEXICAN REVOLUTION
    Alan Knight
MICROBIOLOGY Nicholas P. Money
MICROBIOMES Angela E. Douglas
MICROECONOMICS Avinash Dixit
MICROSCOPY Terence Allen
THE MIDDLE AGES Miri Rubin
MILITARY JUSTICE Eugene R. Fidell
MILITARY STRATEGY
    Antulio J. Echevarria II
JOHN STUART MILL Gregory Claeys
MINERALS David Vaughan
MIRACLES Yujin Nagasawa
MODERN ARCHITECTURE
    Adam Sharr
MODERN ART David Cottington
MODERN BRAZIL Anthony W. Pereira
MODERN CHINA Rana Mitter
MODERN DRAMA
    Kirsten E. Shepherd-Barr
MODERN FRANCE
    Vanessa R. Schwartz
MODERN INDIA Craig Jeffrey
MODERN IRELAND Senia Pašeta
MODERN ITALY Anna Cento Bull

MODERN JAPAN
  Christopher Goto-Jones
MODERN LATIN AMERICAN
  LITERATURE
  Roberto González Echevarría
MODERN WAR Richard English
MODERNISM Christopher Butler
MOLECULAR BIOLOGY Aysha Divan
  and Janice A. Royds
MOLECULES Philip Ball
MONASTICISM Stephen J. Davis
THE MONGOLS Morris Rossabi
MONTAIGNE William M. Hamlin
MOONS David A. Rothery
MORMONISM Richard Lyman Bushman
MOUNTAINS Martin F. Price
MUHAMMAD Jonathan A. C. Brown
MULTICULTURALISM Ali Rattansi
MULTILINGUALISM John C. Maher
MUSIC Nicholas Cook
MUSIC AND TECHNOLOGY
  Mark Katz
MYTH Robert A. Segal
NANOTECHNOLOGY Philip Moriarty
NAPOLEON David A. Bell
THE NAPOLEONIC WARS
  Mike Rapport
NATIONALISM Steven Grosby
NATIVE AMERICAN LITERATURE
  Sean Teuton
NAVIGATION Jim Bennett
NAZI GERMANY Jane Caplan
NEGOTIATION Carrie Menkel-Meadow
NEOLIBERALISM Manfred B. Steger
  and Ravi K. Roy
NETWORKS Guido Caldarelli and
  Michele Catanzaro
THE NEW TESTAMENT
  Luke Timothy Johnson
THE NEW TESTAMENT AS
  LITERATURE Kyle Keefer
NEWTON Robert Iliffe
NIETZSCHE Michael Tanner
NINETEENTH-CENTURY BRITAIN
  Christopher Harvie and
  H. C. G. Matthew
THE NORMAN CONQUEST
  George Garnett
NORTH AMERICAN INDIANS
  Theda Perdue and Michael D. Green

NORTHERN IRELAND
  Marc Mulholland
NOTHING Frank Close
NUCLEAR PHYSICS Frank Close
NUCLEAR POWER Maxwell Irvine
NUCLEAR WEAPONS
  Joseph M. Siracusa
NUMBER THEORY Robin Wilson
NUMBERS Peter M. Higgins
NUTRITION David A. Bender
OBJECTIVITY Stephen Gaukroger
OBSERVATIONAL ASTRONOMY
  Geoff Cottrell
OCEANS Dorrik Stow
THE OLD TESTAMENT
  Michael D. Coogan
THE ORCHESTRA D. Kern Holoman
ORGANIC CHEMISTRY
  Graham Patrick
ORGANIZATIONS Mary Jo Hatch
ORGANIZED CRIME
  Georgios A. Antonopoulos and
  Georgios Papanicolaou
ORTHODOX CHRISTIANITY
  A. Edward Siecienski
OVID Llewelyn Morgan
PAGANISM Owen Davies
PAKISTAN Pippa Virdee
THE PALESTINIAN-ISRAELI
  CONFLICT Martin Bunton
PANDEMICS Christian W. McMillen
PARTICLE PHYSICS Frank Close
PAUL E. P. Sanders
IVAN PAVLOV Daniel P. Todes
PEACE Oliver P. Richmond
PENTECOSTALISM William K. Kay
PERCEPTION Brian Rogers
THE PERIODIC TABLE Eric R. Scerri
PHILOSOPHICAL METHOD
  Timothy Williamson
PHILOSOPHY Edward Craig
PHILOSOPHY IN THE ISLAMIC
  WORLD Peter Adamson
PHILOSOPHY OF BIOLOGY
  Samir Okasha
PHILOSOPHY OF LAW Raymond Wacks
PHILOSOPHY OF MIND
  Barbara Gail Montero
PHILOSOPHY OF PHYSICS
  David Wallace

PHILOSOPHY OF SCIENCE
Samir Okasha
PHILOSOPHY OF RELIGION
Tim Bayne
PHOTOGRAPHY Steve Edwards
PHYSICAL CHEMISTRY Peter Atkins
PHYSICS Sidney Perkowitz
PILGRIMAGE Ian Reader
PLAGUE Paul Slack
PLANETARY SYSTEMS
Raymond T. Pierrehumbert
PLANETS David A. Rothery
PLANTS Timothy Walker
PLATE TECTONICS Peter Molnar
SYLVIA PLATH Heather Clark
PLATO Julia Annas
POETRY Bernard O'Donoghue
POLITICAL PHILOSOPHY David Miller
POLITICS Kenneth Minogue
POLYGAMY Sarah M. S. Pearsall
POPULISM Cas Mudde and
Cristóbal Rovira Kaltwasser
POSTCOLONIALISM
Robert J. C. Young
POSTMODERNISM Christopher Butler
POSTSTRUCTURALISM
Catherine Belsey
POVERTY Philip N. Jefferson
PREHISTORY Chris Gosden
PRESOCRATIC PHILOSOPHY
Catherine Osborne
PRIVACY Raymond Wacks
PROBABILITY John Haigh
PROGRESSIVISM Walter Nugent
PROHIBITION W. J. Rorabaugh
PROJECTS Andrew Davies
PROTESTANTISM Mark A. Noll
MARCEL PROUST Joshua Landy
PSEUDOSCIENCE Michael D. Gordin
PSYCHIATRY Tom Burns
PSYCHOANALYSIS Daniel Pick
PSYCHOLINGUISTICS
Ferenda Ferreria
PSYCHOLOGY Gillian Butler and
Freda McManus
PSYCHOLOGY OF MUSIC
Elizabeth Hellmuth Margulis
PSYCHOPATHY Essi Viding
PSYCHOTHERAPY Tom Burns and
Eva Burns-Lundgren

PUBLIC ADMINISTRATION
Stella Z. Theodoulou and Ravi K. Roy
PUBLIC HEALTH Virginia Berridge
PURITANISM Francis J. Bremer
THE QUAKERS Pink Dandelion
QUANTUM THEORY
John Polkinghorne
RACISM Ali Rattansi
RADIOACTIVITY Claudio Tuniz
RASTAFARI Ennis B. Edmonds
READING Belinda Jack
THE REAGAN REVOLUTION Gil Troy
REALITY Jan Westerhoff
RECONSTRUCTION Allen C. Guelzo
THE REFORMATION Peter Marshall
REFUGEES Gil Loescher
RELATIVITY Russell Stannard
RELIGION Thomas A. Tweed
RELIGION IN AMERICA Timothy Beal
THE RENAISSANCE Jerry Brotton
RENAISSANCE ART
Geraldine A. Johnson
RENEWABLE ENERGY Nick Jelley
REPTILES T. S. Kemp
REVOLUTIONS Jack A. Goldstone
RHETORIC Richard Toye
RISK Baruch Fischhoff and John Kadvany
RITUAL Barry Stephenson
RIVERS Nick Middleton
ROBOTICS Alan Winfield
ROCKS Jan Zalasiewicz
ROMAN BRITAIN Peter Salway
THE ROMAN EMPIRE
Christopher Kelly
THE ROMAN REPUBLIC
David M. Gwynn
ROMANTICISM Michael Ferber
ROUSSEAU Robert Wokler
THE RULE OF LAW Aziz Z. Huq
RUSSELL A. C. Grayling
THE RUSSIAN ECONOMY
Richard Connolly
RUSSIAN HISTORY Geoffrey Hosking
RUSSIAN LITERATURE Catriona Kelly
RUSSIAN POLITICS Brian D. Taylor
THE RUSSIAN REVOLUTION
S. A. Smith
SAINTS Simon Yarrow
SAMURAI Michael Wert
SAVANNAS Peter A. Furley

SCEPTICISM Duncan Pritchard
SCHIZOPHRENIA Chris Frith and
Eve Johnstone
SCHOPENHAUER
Christopher Janaway
SCIENCE AND RELIGION
Thomas Dixon and Adam R. Shapiro
SCIENCE FICTION David Seed
THE SCIENTIFIC REVOLUTION
Lawrence M. Principe
SCOTLAND Rab Houston
SECULARISM Andrew Copson
THE SELF Marya Schechtman
SEXUAL SELECTION Marlene Zuk and
Leigh W. Simmons
SEXUALITY Véronique Mottier
WILLIAM SHAKESPEARE
Stanley Wells
SHAKESPEARE'S COMEDIES
Bart van Es
SHAKESPEARE'S SONNETS
AND POEMS Jonathan F. S. Post
SHAKESPEARE'S TRAGEDIES
Stanley Wells
GEORGE BERNARD SHAW
Christopher Wixson
MARY SHELLEY Charlotte Gordon
THE SHORT STORY Andrew Kahn
SIKHISM Eleanor Nesbitt
SILENT FILM Donna Kornhaber
THE SILK ROAD James A. Millward
SLANG Jonathon Green
SLEEP Steven W. Lockley and
Russell G. Foster
SMELL Matthew Cobb
ADAM SMITH Christopher J. Berry
SOCIAL AND CULTURAL
ANTHROPOLOGY
John Monaghan and Peter Just
SOCIALISM Michael Newman
SOCIAL PSYCHOLOGY Richard J. Crisp
SOCIAL SCIENCE Alexander Betts
SOCIAL WORK Sally Holland and
Jonathan Scourfield
SOCIOLINGUISTICS John Edwards
SOCIOLOGY Steve Bruce
SOCRATES C. C. W. Taylor
SOFT MATTER Tom McLeish
SOPHOCLES Edith Hall
SOUND Mike Goldsmith

SOUTHEAST ASIA James R. Rush
THE SOVIET UNION Stephen Lovell
THE SPANISH CIVIL WAR
Helen Graham
SPANISH LITERATURE Jo Labanyi
THE SPARTANS Andrew J. Bayliss
SPINOZA Roger Scruton
SPIRITUALITY Philip Sheldrake
SPORT Mike Cronin
STARS Andrew King
STATISTICS David J. Hand
STEM CELLS Jonathan Slack
STOICISM Brad Inwood
STRUCTURAL ENGINEERING
David Blockley
STUART BRITAIN John Morrill
SUBURBS Carl Abbott
THE SUN Philip Judge
SUPERCONDUCTIVITY
Stephen Blundell
SUPERSTITION Stuart Vyse
SURVEILLANCE David Lyon
SUSTAINABILITY Saleem Ali
SYMBIOSIS Nancy A. Moran
SYMMETRY Ian Stewart
SYNAESTHESIA Julia Simner
SYNTHETIC BIOLOGY Jamie A. Davies
SYSTEMS BIOLOGY Eberhard O. Voit
TAXATION Stephen Smith
TEETH Peter S. Ungar
TERRORISM Charles Townshend
THEATRE Marvin Carlson
THEOLOGY David F. Ford
THINKING AND REASONING
Jonathan St B. T. Evans
HENRY DAVID THOREAU
Lawrence Buell
THOUGHT Tim Bayne
THUCYDIDES Jennifer T. Roberts
TIBETAN BUDDHISM
Matthew T. Kapstein
TIDES David George Bowers and
Emyr Martyn Roberts
TIME Jenann Ismael
TOCQUEVILLE Harvey C. Mansfield
TOLERATION Andrew Murphy
J. R. R. TOLKIEN Matthew Townend
LEO TOLSTOY Liza Knapp
TOPOLOGY Richard Earl
TRAGEDY Adrian Poole

TRANSLATION Matthew Reynolds
THE TREATY OF VERSAILLES
Michael S. Neiberg
TRIGONOMETRY
Glen Van Brummelen
THE TROJAN WAR Eric H. Cline
ANTHONY TROLLOPE Dinah Birch
TRUST Katherine Hawley
THE TUDORS John Guy
TWENTIETH-CENTURY BRITAIN
Kenneth O. Morgan
TYPOGRAPHY Paul Luna
THE UNITED NATIONS
Jussi M. Hanhimäki
UNIVERSITIES AND COLLEGES
David Palfreyman and Paul Temple
THE U.S. CIVIL WAR Louis P. Masur
THE U.S. CONGRESS Donald A. Ritchie
THE U.S. CONSTITUTION
David J. Bodenhamer
THE U.S. SUPREME COURT
Linda Greenhouse
UTILITARIANISM
Katarzyna de Lazari-Radek and
Peter Singer
UTOPIANISM Lyman Tower Sargent
VATICAN II Shaun Blanchard and
Stephen Bullivant
VETERINARY SCIENCE James Yeates
THE VICTORIANS Martin Hewitt
THE VIKINGS Julian D. Richards

VIOLENCE Philip Dwyer
THE VIRGIN MARY
Mary Joan Winn Leith
THE VIRTUES Craig A. Boyd and
Kevin Timpe
VIRUSES Dorothy H. Crawford
VOLCANOES Michael J. Branney and
Jan Zalasiewicz
VOLTAIRE Nicholas Cronk
WAR AND RELIGION Jolyon Mitchell
and Joshua Rey
WAR AND TECHNOLOGY Alex Roland
WATER John Finney
WAVES Mike Goldsmith
WEATHER Storm Dunlop
SIMONE WEIL
A. Rebecca Rozelle-Stone
THE WELFARE STATE David Garland
WITCHCRAFT Malcolm Gaskill
WITTGENSTEIN A. C. Grayling
WORK Stephen Fineman
WORLD MUSIC Philip Bohlman
WORLD MYTHOLOGY
David Leeming
THE WORLD TRADE
ORGANIZATION Amrita Narlikar
WORLD WAR II Gerhard L. Weinberg
WRITING AND SCRIPT
Andrew Robinson
ZIONISM Michael Stanislawski
ÉMILE ZOLA Brian Nelson

Available soon:

MATHEMATICAL BIOLOGY
Philip Maini
AGATHA CHRISTIE Gill Plain

HUMAN GEOGRAPHY Patricia Daley
and Ian Klinke

For more information visit our website
www.oup.com/vsi/

Ross Brann

MOSES MAIMONIDES

A Very Short Introduction

Oxford University Press is a department of the University of Oxford.
It furthers the University's objective of excellence in research, scholarship,
and education by publishing worldwide. Oxford is a registered trade mark of
Oxford University Press in the UK and in certain other countries.

Published in the United States of America by Oxford University Press
198 Madison Avenue, New York, NY 10016, United States of America.

© Oxford University Press 2025

All rights reserved. No part of this publication may be reproduced, stored in a retrieval system, transmitted, used for text and data mining, or used for training artificial intelligence, in any form or by any means, without the prior permission in writing of Oxford University Press, or as expressly permitted by law, by license or under terms agreed with the appropriate reprographics rights organization. Inquiries concerning reproduction outside the scope of the above should be sent to the Rights Department, Oxford University Press, at the address above.

You must not circulate this work in any other form
and you must impose this same condition on any acquirer.

Library of Congress Cataloging-in-Publication Data
Names: Brann, Ross, 1949- author.
Title: Moses Maimonides : a very short introduction / Ross Brann.
Description: First edition. | New York : Oxford University Press, 2025. |
Includes bibliographical references and index.
Identifiers: LCCN 2024060211 (print) | LCCN 2024060212 (ebook) |
ISBN 9780197536988 (paperback) | ISBN 9780197537008 (epub)
Subjects: LCSH: Maimonides, Moses, 1135-1204. | Maimonides, Moses,
1135-1204—Teachings. | Rabbis—Egypt—Biography. |
Jewish philosophers—Egypt—Biography. | Jewish scholars—Egypt—Biography.
Classification: LCC BM755.M6 B69 2025 (print) | LCC BM755.M6 (ebook) |
DDC 296.1/81 [B]—dc23/eng/20250209
LC record available at https://lccn.loc.gov/2024060211
LC ebook record available at https://lccn.loc.gov/2024060212

Printed by Integrated Books International, United States of America

The manufacturer's authorized representative in the EU for product safety is
Oxford University Press España S.A., Parque Empresarial San Fernando de Henares,
Avenida de Castilla, 2 - 28830 Madrid (www.oup.es/en).

The manufacturer's authorised representative in the EU for product safety is Oxford University Press España S.A. of El Parque Empresarial San Fernando de Henares, Avenida de Castilla, 2 - 28830 Madrid (www.oup.es/en or product.safety@oup.com). OUP España S.A. also acts as importer into Spain of products made by the manufacturer.

Contents

List of illustrations xvii

Preface xix

Introduction 1

1 Maimonides and his world 6

2 "Back home in the west" 28

3 Loving God with the mind 50

4 The humanistic rabbi, philosopher, physician 78

5 Turning the parochial into the universal 97

6 Maimonides in historical perspective 106

References 117

Further reading 127

Chronology 131

Index 133

List of illustrations

1 Map of the Mediterranean during Maimonides' lifetime **xxii**

2 The Great Mosque of Cordoba **7**
Barone Firenze/Shutterstock

3 Statue of Maimonides in Cordoba **9**
Lmbuga (Luis Miguel Bugallo Sánchez), CC BY-SA 4.0

4 View of Old Fez **14**
Robert Harding Video/Shutterstock

5 Illuminated manuscript of the *Mishneh Torah*, fifteenth-century, Italy **47**
World Digital Library

6 *Sefer Ha-Mitsvot* (*Book of Commandments*), Yemen, 1492 **72**
Scribe: Shalom ben Zechariah Eldani
Hartman Family Collection

7 Ben Ezra Synagogue in Fustat (Old Cairo) **80**
Photo by Fareed Kotb/Anadolu Agency via Getty Images

8 Extract from Maimonides' *Regimen on Health* (1198) **82**
Cambridge University Library T-S AS 152.86
Used with permission of the Syndics of Cambridge University Library

9 An autograph responsum (answer to a legal query) by Maimonides **86**
British Library/Granger, NYC—all rights reserved

10 Relief carving of Maimonides (1950) in the chamber of the House of Representatives, US Capitol **114**
Architect of the Capitol

Preface

Writing about Moses Maimonides is a humbling challenge especially in the form of a very short introduction. Such a larger-than-life subject resists reductive interpretation in virtually all his works and in his person. Maimonidean scholarship abounds as do books about him written for the reading public in English, Spanish, French, German, Arabic, and Hebrew. Until recently, academic monographs and articles tended to focus strictly on Maimonides' biography, rabbinical works, philosophical oeuvre, communal endeavors, or his medical writings separately. Comprehensive studies on Maimonides are apt to follow this model by devoting chapters to each of these discreet subjects.

This very short introduction to Moses Maimonides draws on Maimonidean scholarship in each of his areas of experience and literary activity. It follows current trends in research which present an integrated view of Maimonides as a rabbinic scholar without peer, a philosophically minded deep thinker, religious reformer (who thought of his life's project as *restoring* the authentic meaning and details of the written and oral Torah), communal leader, physician, and scientist who moved seamlessly between specialized, private, and public Jewish and Muslim spheres. Indeed, his written works traverse multiple disciplines and discourses, employ several linguistic registers, voices, and literary genres, and address various audiences. Accordingly, this book organizes Maimonides' thinking and writings thematically by way of suggestive "chapter headings," to use one his catch phrases in *The Guide of the Perplexed* (although not in the sense of enigmas and puzzles to be deciphered) and puts his works into dialogue with one another intertextually.

My sincere thanks to the two blind proposal readers at the outset of this project and the blind readers of the completed manuscript draft who offered helpful suggestions, extremely valuable criticism, and important corrections to various overstatements and mistakes, to my advanced students at Cornell University who have studied Maimonides with me, to my project editors par excellence Nancy Toff and Rada Radojicic, to Thomas Deva, who meticulously managed production of the book, to Robin Reid for excellent copyediting, and to Melissa Hyde for preparing the index with such great professional care. Of course, I am responsible for any remaining errors of omission or commission. Accolades are due my partner for life, Eileen Yagoda, for absolutely everything. I dedicate this book to our six-year-old granddaughter, Talia, whose voracious appetite for books and instinctive, irrepressible drive for exploration, discovery, and reflection would, I think, impress Maimonides.

Moses Maimonides

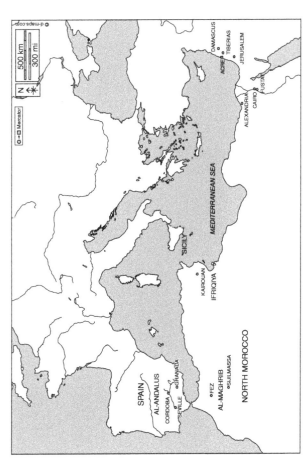

1. Map of the Islamic Mediterranean during Maimonides' lifetime in the 10th–13th centuries.

Introduction

Maimonides is generally regarded as the predominant Jewish figure of the premodern age. He is variously known in Jewish history as Moses Maimonides (his Latinized name), Moshe ben Maimon, *Rambam* (the Hebrew acronym for Rabbi Moses ben Maimon), "the Great Rav in Israel," "the Great Eagle" (Ez. 17:3), "the light of the West," and "the second Moses." He always identified himself as "Moses the son of Rabbi Maimon the Sephardi." Islamic sources recognize him, typically with pronounced respect, as Abu 'Imran Musa b. 'Ubayd Allah Maymun al-Qurtubi al-Isra'ili al- al-Andalusi; and Christian scholastics and Hebraists who studied his theological work attentively knew him variously as Rabbi Moyses, Moyses Judaeos, Moyses Aegyptius, *Doctor Dubiorum*, and *Doctor Perplexorum*. For its part, modern scholarship considers at least five Maimonides figures—the Aristotelian philosopher, the physician and scientist, the Jewish religious thinker, the peerless rabbinic scholar and expert on Jewish law, and the communal leader of the Jews of Egypt. It is a sign of his singular genius and renown that modern Spain, Morocco, Egypt (which renovated and rededicated the nineteenth-century Ibn Maymun Synagogue in 2010), Israel, and Sephardi Jews at large all lay claim to him.

Maimonides was also a controversial figure in some quarters. His humanistic, rational, and philosophically inspired understanding of the Hebrew Bible and rabbinic tradition did not find universal favor among Jewish communities of Christian Castile, Catalonia, Tzarfat (France), and Ashkenaz (Central and Eastern Europe). Among those who doubted him, however, his works were influential and elicited a reckoning that proved transformative even among rabbinic traditionalists, pietists, and mystics. Today, observant Jews who follow Ashkenazi rabbinic tradition hold in esteem Maimonides' supreme mastery of the details and intricacies of the Torah in its most capacious sense, the totality of the Hebrew Bible—the written law—and rabbinic tradition—the oral Torah. They accept Maimonides' rabbinic works as pillars of the Jewish canon for study but do not follow his rulings uniformly and do not subscribe at all to his intellectual ethos. Indeed, some endeavor to subvert it.

It is fortunate that the survival of Moses Maimonides' formal letters, private correspondence, and documents in the Cairo Geniza (some sixty autograph fragments) along with references to him in Jewish and Islamic texts, enable us to appreciate the fullness of the man—the doting father, the bereaved older brother accountable for his family's wellbeing, the sensitive pastoral counselor and expert on Jewish law, the skilled and sought-after physician who served the wider public in Fustat (Old Cairo) and the sultan's court in Cairo, the influential Jewish communal leader with an acute sense of social responsibility, the towering public figure, as well as the illustrious rabbinic scholar, intellectual visionary, and mentor to exceptional students. Yet more than eight centuries after his death the meaning of his life and work remains as contested as ever, as readers find contradictions in Maimonides' writings through the parallax view of their respective disciplinary, ideological, or historical lenses. To whom does Maimonides properly belong? What did he represent during particular historical periods and how has understanding of his figure changed over the course of time?

2

Until relatively recently the tendency among his readers has been to compartmentalize Maimonides' work according to supposedly distinct branches of learning. These disciplines, however, are cultural products of the nineteenth and twentieth centuries and are problematic when applied to the world of classical Islam (the Middle Ages of Christendom) with its own disciplinary divisions—grammar, logic, and rhetoric; arithmetic, geometry, and astronomy; the natural sciences and metaphysics; and the canonical texts of each religious community. Maimonides mastered them all at an early age.

Nevertheless, some modern scholars have treated his rabbinic works and discussed Maimonides primarily within the context of the history of *halakha* (Jewish law). Others have studied his theological works and viewed Maimonides primarily in the context of the history of Jewish thought while acknowledging the presence of external "influences" in his work. In that intellectual sphere alone, experts have regarded Maimonides primarily a philosopher or alternatively as strictly a Jewish theologian. All such tensions in the study of a singular and monumental figure in the history of Jewish tradition and thought, as well as a scholar whose life and work belong as much to Islamic civilization as to Jewish history, culture, and practice persist in some quarters.

Thankfully, intellectual historians have surmounted the difficulties posed by the temporal distance between Maimonides' times and our own as well as the disciplinary partitions in the modern history of Maimonidean scholarship. This integrative turn in Maimonidean studies examines the interrelatedness of all Maimonides' intellectual, literary, professional, and communal ventures. It presents Maimonides in his historical context across intellectual, religious, and social boundaries; that is, it reads Maimonides as a figure in cultural history as he was probably read within the multiple contexts in which he wrote and within which his various audiences, students, readers, and colleagues and critics encountered him.

Although Maimonides endeavored to solve for once and for all various monumental problems he confronted by restoring the original but lost significance and details of the Torah, his analytic perspective was also keenly attuned to the variability of history and society. The key to engaging Maimonides on his own terms is to understand that he applied a rational, anthropological-historical intellectual regimen characteristic of his scientific research and subsequent medical practices to his life's work in all its dimensions. He observed and studied a problem, diagnosed it, and then prescribed and administered a remedy for it, whether the concern was physical, metaphysical, spiritual, intellectual, or social in nature.

Already in the *Epistle on Forced Conversion* (also known as the *Epistle on Martyrdom* or the *Epistle on the Sanctification of the [Divine] Name*) composed between 1160 and 1165, Maimonides framed his counsel for the beleaguered Jews of al-Andalus and the Maghrib by gesturing to this therapeutic method: "Realizing this amazing matter that hurts the eyes, I undertook to gather pharmaceutics and roots from the books of the ancients, of which I intend to prepare medicine and salve helpful for this sickness, and heal it with the help of God." Similarly, the "The Eight Chapters" in the *Commentary on the Mishnah*, completed around 1168, avers: "the improvement of the moral qualities is brought about by the healing of the soul and its activities. Therefore, just as the physician, who endeavors to cure the human body, must have perfect knowledge of it in its entirety and its individual parts, just as he must know what causes sickness that it may be avoided, and must also be acquainted with the means by which a patient may be cured, so likewise, he who tries to cure the soul, wishing to improve the moral qualities, must have a knowledge of the soul in its totality and its parts, must know how to prevent it from becoming diseased, and how to maintain its health."

Judah al-Harizi, one of his translators and enthusiasts, encapsulated Maimonides' curative identity in a poem of praise:

> He was named Musa ('the healer') for through him the Torah heals,
> For he became a panacea for all ills.
> He resuscitated the sciences and wounds mended,
> The sick, who ceased to ail, he tended.

For Moses, then, the diagnostic and remedial method was no mere metaphor for confronting what ailed the body or soul of a person or society. Rather, Maimonides' scientific-philosophical perspective on human existence defined his understanding of the Torah's purpose in regulating individual wellbeing, communal welfare, and social good that was his abiding concern and life's mission. Torah, science, and philosophy conjointly guide one and all in a redemptive quest for enlightenment and toward a life of human perfection.

Chapter 1
Maimonides and his world

Cordoba, Maimonides' birthplace (1138), was the intellectual center of al-Andalus (Islamic Spain) and the largest metropolis on the European continent. Since the mid-eighth century Cordoba served as the capital of an Umayyad Andalusi emirate that was politically autonomous yet economically and culturally connected to the eastern centers of Islamdom. Tenth-century Cordoba, now capital of the unified, independent Umayyad Andalusi caliphate at the height of its powers and affluence, acquired the reputation among outsiders such as the Saxon poet Hrotsvit of Gandersheim as the "ornament of the world." Its monumental architecture, decorative artistry, cleanliness, economic vitality, cultural sophistication, and renown as the home of religious and scientific scholarship and literary creativity mesmerized visitors and those abroad who received reports of its magnificent splendor.

Members of the small Jewish minority community (and Andalusi Christians to a lesser degree) in this center of civilization contributed to these cultural and intellectual ventures with their Muslim counterparts. In some instances, Jews participated alongside them during a two-century-long period modern Jewish historiography styled "the Golden Age of the Jews in Spain" and more recently and less problematically "the Golden Age of Jewish culture" in "Islamic Spain" (al-Andalus).

2. The Great Mosque of Cordoba is an outstanding monument of Andalusi architecture with its expansive, geometrically designed prayer hall. It was constructed in 786 and enlarged during the ninth and tenth centuries.

The unified Andalusi state collapsed in the eleventh century and was replaced by competing "party kingdoms" (1009–86). Cordoba, a ministate itself as of 1031, remained a center of Jewish life. Following that culturally productive but politically turbulent period in a land divided against itself by internecine rivalries, a dynasty of North African Berbers, the Almoravids, extended their rule to al-Andalus in 1090. They crossed into the peninsula at the request of the Andalusi Muslims, in part to protect the land from the growing strength and territorial ambitions of the northern Iberian Christian kingdoms. Indeed, Castile under Alfonso VI conquered Toledo, in the center of the peninsula, in 1085. The Jews generally benefitted from the stability the Almoravids restored to al-Andalus, and the "Golden Age" of Jewish culture in Iberia continued into the twelfth century.

Maimonides' father, Maimon ben Joseph, was an accomplished rabbinic scholar, judge, and biblical exegete from an eminent family of sages going back seven generations, according to Maimonides' reckoning. Maimon studied at the celebrated rabbinical academy in Lucena with Joseph (ha-Levi ben Meir) ibn Migash, the fabled religious authority of the Jews of Sepharad (alternate spelling: Sefarad), the Hebrew name for al-Andalus and thereafter for the entire Iberian peninsula. Maimonides later would refer to Ibn Migash as "my teacher" and he frequently cited R. Isaac ben Jacob al-Fasi, R. Joseph's august predecessor at the academy, as the revered figure of Andalusi rabbinic scholars. Maimon naturally served as Moses' first teacher and the principal conduit for transmitting the Sephardi halakhic tradition that was the foundation of Andalusi Jewish life. On multiple occasions Maimonides testified that his own intellectual orientation, legal judgments, and opinions were informed by his father's teachings and, through them, the accumulated wisdom of the Jews of al-Andalus.

In 1148, when Moses was a young lad, Almoravid Morocco and subsequently al-Andalus were overrun by the Almohads, another North African Berber dynasty of Islamic revivalists. Medieval Arabic chronicles report that the Almohads were religious revolutionaries who prohibited the public practice of any religion in their united Andalusi-Maghribi kingdom other than the peculiar interpretation and practice of Islam they imposed as a "universal religion." To that end they compelled the Almoravids and other Muslim opponents to accept Almohad Islam or be put to death. Arabic sources also relate that Christian and Jewish minorities who did not flee the country but remained in the realm were subject to forced conversions to Almohad Islam or executed, a policy then virtually without precedent and contrary to the Qur'an (2:256) and its interpretation in Islamic law. Jewish literary sources and a letter discovered in the Cairo Geniza paint a picture of the upheaval and persecution as the most recent in an extended chain of catastrophes inflicted on the Jews in the lands of their diaspora ever since the early Roman period. A letter by the

3. A statue of Maimonides in Cordoba, the city of his birth and youth, is situated in the historic Jewish area of the city. A facsimile of his autograph is set into the base.

merchant Solomon ben Judah al-Sijilmasi in Fustat (Old Cairo) dated 1148 and a passage from a text by the physician and scholar Joseph ben Judah ibn 'Aqnin from Barcelona living in Fez provide explicit reports of the very specific travails engulfing the Jews of the Islamic West. Nevertheless, some Jews remained in al-Andalus and dissembled as crypto-Jews or pseudo-Muslims. In effect they practiced what Islam refers to as *taqiyya*—religious dissimulation under acute duress—that foreshadowed one of the Jewish responses to a century of coerced conversions to Catholicism in Christian Spain from 1391 to 1492.

Unlike many Andalusi Jews who headed for sanctuary in Christian Castile, R. Maimon and his household, which included Moses' younger brother, David, and apparently two sisters, seem to have trekked around al-Andalus in search of relative safety and refuge. R. Maimon somehow managed to continue to provide young Moses with a comprehensive rabbinic education, along with advanced instruction in scientific and philosophical subjects. Although the work's authenticity is still disputed by a minority of scholars, Maimonides seems to have written his first publication, *Treatise on the Art of Logic*, when he was only sixteen years old. Addressed to a figure learned in Jewish law and in Arabic eloquence, the work presents a review of the rudiments of logical terminology and includes a chapter on the classification of the sciences, from the theoretical to the practical. Elsewhere Maimonides mentions having read texts with the sons of an important Muslim astronomer and a prominent Muslim philosopher in Seville. The budding sage of only twenty next produced a rudimentary study of the intricacies of the Jewish lunisolar liturgical calendar, the *Treatise on Lunar Intercalation*. Maimonides later would draw on the advanced mathematical and astronomical knowledge informing this early work in his elaborate and definitive legal treatment of the subject, "Laws of the Sanctification of the New Moon," in the *Code of Jewish Law*, known as the *Mishneh Torah*.

Conditions under the Almohads seem to have varied between cities, and the dynasty's harsh policies toward its Jewish subjects may have been implemented in stages, perhaps accounting for the Maimon family's checkered movements within al-Andalus. At first, the situation was more severe in Morocco than on the peninsula. Within a generation the circumstances for Jews seem to have improved in the former after the dynasty's founder 'Abd al-Mu'min (r. 1130–63) consolidated power and required the administrative experience of Jewish and Christian civil servants in operating the state bureaucracy. The Maimon family thus fled al-Andalus around 1159 for Almohad Fez, long the spiritual center of the Maghrib (North Africa) for Jews and Muslims alike and a major center of Islamic learning. Once there Maimon authored an important *Epistle of Consolation* (1159–60) designed to encourage the besieged crypto-Jewish communities under Almohad rule and to dissuade its embattled members from succumbing to despair or the lure of a false messiah during a time of extreme crisis. In short order Moses would embrace his father's compassionate teaching and rabbinic rulings regarding how Jews might persevere in secret when persecution overwhelmed them.

The situation in Morocco reverted to its previously perilous state for Jews under 'Abd al-Mu'min's son and successor, Abu Ya'qub Yusuf (r. 1163–84). Indirect evidence suggests and direct testimony from Arabic sources reports that Maimon's family lived for years in al-Andalus and in Fez as pseudo-Muslims—outwardly feigning adherence to Islam while secretly abiding by Jewish law. These formative experiences left a profound mark on Moses that is evident in his formal and informal communications as a communal leader and authority. In his *Epistle on Apostasy*, in effect a companion piece to his father's *Letter of Consolation* addressed to the Maghribi Jewish community, Maimonides responded to a missive from a troubled North African Jew with systematic and detailed guidance. His bewildered correspondent cites a contemporary rabbinic authority living beyond Almohad dominion who denounced crypto-Jews as irredeemable apostates. Refuting said "expert," Moses relates that he is "well informed regarding the issue, and...not ignorant of it as this man is...." Maimonides urges this supplicant and the implied larger audience in a similar position to leave the country for safer lands: "What I counsel myself, and what I should like to suggest to all my friends and everyone that consults me, is to leave these places and go to where he can practice religion and fulfill the Law without compulsion or fear." For those who could not leave the country or declined to martyr themselves he instructed that it is permissible to utter the profession of Islamic faith in public while abiding by Jewish practices in secret in order to preserve life: "But in this persecution to which we are subjected we do not pretend that we are idolators, we only appear to believe what they assert. They fully understand that we do not mean it at all, and are simply deceiving their ruler.... This compulsion imposes no action only speech. They know very well that we do not mean what we say, and that what we say is only to escape the ruler's punishment and to satisfy him with this simple confession."

Here was the first inkling that Moses, already a brilliant young religious intellectual who doubtlessly sought solitude for study and contemplation, would devote the public face of his life to sympathetically caring for his religious community at the expense of his intellectual regimen and inner life. But there was another side to his personality to which he freely admitted. Maimonides later confessed to his favorite disciple that he was intemperate as a young man: "When I was your age and even older than you, I was more vehement than you. I would wield my tongue and pen against great and wise men when they sought to disagree with me." Indeed, many of Maimonides' works direct his impatient rancor toward foolish, misinformed, or ignorant "experts."

In Almohad Fez, Maimonides continued to delve deeply into philosophy and science, carried on with his study of medicine, and sought training as a physician with senior medical authorities.

Somehow Moses persisted in his surreptitious study of Torah during this period. Joseph ibn 'Aqnin, who likely came into contact with Maimonides in Fez, cites Moses' rabbinic scholarship as a sign of the miraculous vitality of Jewish intellectual endeavor and achievement produced in secret under duress and in danger. It refers, he wrote to the "period of forcible conversion during which we fulfill the precepts of the Law at the point of the sword, and particularly this persecution of ours [the Almohads'], may the Lord put an end to it. Yet, as is well known, we steadily engage in the study of Torah. The clearest proof of our statement is the presence in our age of the great sage...Moses...son of...Maimon in Fez, whose rank in learning is unique, and whose works testify to his learning....This is in addition to the superiority he enjoys in the various fields of science. If he were the only appropriate example during the persecution, it would be ample [proof]."

While engaging in clandestine Torah study, Maimonides intensified his reading of Islamic law and thought and became fully versed in both courses of study. His mastery of Islamic sources, including Maliki (the school of Islamic law predominant in the Islamic West) and Almohad law and doctrine, served as an inspiration for the epic, canonical work he would undertake in the systematic articulation of Jewish law and thought, the *Mishneh Torah*. In 1161 he commenced work on his first major composition and first book of Jewish religious law, the *Commentary on the Mishnah*. Seven difficult years in the making, the *Commentary* displayed Maimonides' complete mastery of the *Mishnah*, the foundational document of rabbinic law dating from 200 CE. Furthermore, the *Commentary* demonstrated what would become Moses' signature intellectual achievement by fusing the *Mishnah*'s legal stipulations with philosophical principles.

After five years in Fez, Maimonides' family (a sister named Miriam remained in the Islamic West and later corresponded with Moses on a matter involving her son) finally escaped Almohad territory for the Levant in 1165, arriving first in Acre. Maimonides

4. Old Fez, where Maimonides' family lived for a time, was an important center of Islamic civilization with its institutions of higher learning and commercial activity. The still-preserved medieval city is notable for its extraordinary density.

continued to labor on the *Commentary on the Mishnah*. He persisted despite the immense risk posed by covertly engaging in rabbinic research in Fez followed by the grueling conditions imposed by the treacherous shipboard voyage across the Mediterranean to the land of Israel. During the same period, Maimonides worked on the closely related *Book of Commandments*, which enumerates and formulates the defining principles of the 613 divine prescriptions and injunctions that comprise the biblical strata of Jewish holy law. Palestine was under Crusader jurisdiction at the time and extremely perilous for Jews, so the family remained in the Holy Land for only a year. They left following a pilgrimage to Jerusalem that Maimonides described as fraught with peril.

The household found refuge in Egypt (1166) under the Fatimids, a (Shiʻi) dynasty known for its relative openness toward Jews and for its patronage of scientific research, culture, and institutions of advanced Islamic studies. Following a brief stay in Alexandria, Maimonides' family settled in Old Cairo (Fustat), home to a prominent Jewish community where Moses would remain for the second half of his life. He reports that his early years in Egypt were especially difficult. His father died, apparently soon after they arrived in Egypt, leaving Moses as head of the household and responsible for his sister and brother. According to a contemporary Muslim biographer of physicians, Maimonides first earned a living by trading in gems while teaching science and philosophy. Eventually, Moses' fortunes improved significantly. He wed the daughter of a physician and government official from a prominent Egyptian Jewish family of scholars, physicians, and communal leaders. In turn Moses' sister married Maimonides' bride's brother. These marital bonds stationed him securely among the local Jewish elites despite his foreign background and Andalusi intellectual orientation.

Maimonides' successful efforts in raising funds for the release of ransomed Crusader captives, overseeing synagogues and communal endowments to support pious activities and his increasing renown as a peerless authority on Jewish law eventually catapulted him to prominence in Egypt and beyond. Jewish communal authorities and scholars from Provence to Yemen would seek his advice, legal rulings, and theological opinions. One of his earliest literary endeavors, the *Epistle to Yemen* (1172), involved the unusual plight of the Jews of Yemen, whose community found itself tormented under the yoke of Zaydi Shi'a rule. The *Epistle to Yemen* is but one of many letters and formal compositions revealing Maimonides' boundless empathy, religious humanism, acute sense of responsibility for the welfare of others, commitment to multiple forms of public service, and uncommon capacity to craft his messages in various linguistic, intellectual, and literary registers depending on the capacity of his addressees. The *Epistle*'s introduction strikes a note of the author's profound humility like that of his unassuming biblical namesake, the prophet Moses. Maimonides' self-effacing comment stands in counterpoint to his renown in Yemen referenced by his correspondent: "They merely expressed their affection for me, speaking and writing in their kindness and goodness.... I am one of the least of the sages of Spain whose adornment has been stripped [see Exod. 33:5] in Exile. Ever vigilant in my studies, I have not attained the learning of my ancestors. How can the Law become lucid to an exile from city to city and from country to country.... Now I have stayed home for a while. If not for the Lord who was with us [Ps. 124:1] and for what our fathers have told us [Ps. 78:3], I would not have collected the little I did and from which I constantly bestow."

A personal letter discovered in the Cairo Geniza further testifies to the gentle, even affable human side of the sage who already seemed larger than life. In it, the document's author, accompanied by his young son, describes his visit with Maimonides to deliver another dignitary's letter. To his astonished delight, Moses' visitor is invited inside the home to partake of refreshment and discuss the letter's contents. The guest proceeds to report in amazement

("Then there transpired that which a book would prove insufficient to describe") that he watched the great Rabbi laugh and play with the man's child alongside Moses' own son, Abraham. Another Geniza letter sent to Maimonides attests to the author's deep affection and reverence for its recipient. Even allowing for the cultural predisposition to frame personal correspondence with compound honorifics, this document provides the reader with a sense of Maimonides' unique stature and the love those in his circle and others who came into direct contact with Moses felt for him. It begins: "His eminent dignity—diadem of glory, our master and teacher light of our eyes, breath of our desire, crown of our head and our glory, peerless in his generation, our lord Moses, the great *rav*, the fortress and tower, sign and wonder of the time, from East to West, son of the honorable, great and holy master and teacher of ours Maimon...surely knows [the greatness] of my yearning for him, my delight in seeing him, and my regret for not being near him." Other contemporary sources refer to Maimonides as the "ark of our covenant," "unique in our generation," and "the Nagid [prince] of a people not bereft."

To return to the communal leader and scholar: Maimonides was no stranger to social, political, or religious controversy and had little tolerance for ignorance, stupidity, or arrogance. He became embroiled in an internecine Jewish dispute concerning the position of "Head of the Jews," the official leader of the Egyptian Jewish community confirmed by the Muslim state authorities. The problem involved more than the machinations of a corrupt autocrat, pejoratively named Zuta' ("Mr. Small") in a literary source that also characterizes him as "wicked." The individual in question belonged to the family of leaders of the Palestinian rabbinical academy whose influence over the Egyptian Jewish community was longstanding. The culprit previously held the post of "Head of the Jews" but was replaced, only to connive to depose another person who was in office. In any case, Maimonides led the forces confronting Zuta' and his party and succeeded in ousting him from the position. It seems however, they were unable to rid themselves for good of Zuta' and his supporters. In any event, soon after the immediate affair was resolved, Maimonides, the relative newcomer to the scene, was appointed "Head of the Jews." It was a time of political transition in Egypt and the Levant under the Ayyubids, a new Sunni Islamic dynasty founded by Saladin in 1171. Maimonides served in that formal capacity for several years and then again briefly in the 1190s, representing the Jewish community and its interests to the government. Eventually the office passed on to his son, Abraham, and generations of his descendants.

Maimonides' foray into Egyptian Jewish politics had another dimension apart from confronting the machinations of an individual and his faction. In this instance it involved Maimonides' religious standing as the "Great Rav in Israel" as opposed to the strictly political position of "Head of the Jews." The Jewish community in Egypt was tripartite, that is, comprised of rabbanite Jews who followed Palestinian legal traditions, those who followed Babylonian rabbinic rites, and Karaites ("Scripturalists") who rejected rabbinic oral tradition and authority and followed their own practices, customs, and beliefs predicated solely on literal interpretation of the Hebrew Bible (at least in theory). Egypt and Palestine under the Fatimids and Ayyubids were vibrant centers of Karaite life supported by Karaite merchants who were among the most prosperous members of the Egyptian Jewish community. To the Islamic authorities, Karaites and Rabbanites were all Jews without distinction, each following its own *madhhab* (Ar. for legal school) and responsible for administering their own religious and communal affairs. Egyptian Rabbanites and Karaites had become accustomed to a high degree of social integration that must have seemed completely foreign to Maimonides, an immigrant from the Islamic West, where Karaites were apparently scarce by comparison. The most prominent rabbinic authority in the land inevitably came into conflict with the Karaites over what he perceived as their undue influence and prominence in Egyptian Jewish life. Maimonides' legal rulings regarding rabbanite interactions with Karaites nevertheless demonstrated flexibility and ranged from unqualified rejection on issues such as the laws of family purity to guarded acceptance of interacting with them in other social and economic matters.

Going back to the tenth century, Jewish physicians and scientists achieved social prominence in Islamdom through government service and utilized their access to power in the interests of their religious community. Maimonides joined their ranks and later served as personal physician to the Ayyubid court, where he mixed freely with Muslim political and intellectual elites. Many such figures were well disposed toward him such as the Muslim judge, poet, and literary theorist Abu l-Qasim ibn Sana' l-Mulk. Maimonides did not consider himself a consummate physician, yet his scholarly companion devoted a lyric of conventionally hyperbolic praise to Moses that was preserved in Ibn Sana' l-Mulk's *diwan* (collected poems):

> I think Galen's medical care treats the body alone
>> but that of Abu 'Imran [Moses'] body and mind.
> Were he to treat the times with his knowledge,
>> he'd cure it with knowledge from the malady of ignorance.
> Were the moon to seek him out for medical treatment,
>> it would obtain the perfection it pursues.
> On the day of the full moon, he'd treat it for its freckles
>> and cure it of sickness on the month's last day.

Other prominent Muslim figures also reference Maimonides admiringly. The biographer of physicians and colleague of Moses' son, Abraham, Ibn Abi Usaybi'a, wrote: "Al-Ra'is Musa (Master Musa) was Abu 'Imran Musa ibn Maymun al-Qurtubi, a Jew, learned in the customs of the Jewish people and numbered amongst their religious authorities and most distinguished scholars. In Egypt, he was the head (*al-ra'is*) of their community, for he was peerless in his time in the art of medicine and its practice, and also was versatile in many disciplines and well versed in philosophy. Sultan al-Malik al-Nasir Salah al-Din (Saladin) became aware of him and sought his medical advice, as did Saladin's son, al-Malik al-Afdal 'Ali." Ibn al-Qifti, who may have crossed paths with Maimonides in Cairo, also compiled a biographical dictionary of physicians. He was an intimate confrere with Joseph ben Judah ibn Simon, Maimonides' "esteemed pupil" to whom he dedicated the *Guide of the Perplexed* in one of its three introductions. Joseph probably served as one of Ibn al-Qifti's main sources for his richly detailed entry on Musa in his canonical work. Most notably, al-Qadi al-Fadil, Saladin's trusted confidant, befriended Maimonides and served as his patron, business partner, and protector. When a Muslim jurist from the Islamic West turned up in Cairo and denounced Moses as a Muslim apostate, likely on account of his time as a crypto-Jew, al-Qadi al-Fadil intervened decisively. The charge was dismissed because the Almohad-imposed forced conversions contravened Islamic law. Maimonides himself marveled at his standing among the Ayyubid elites he tended to as a physician. In one of Moses' cluster of letters to his beloved disciple Joseph ben Judah that have come down to us he writes: "I must tell you that I have attained great fame in medicine among the eminent, such as the chief judge, the amirs, the house of al-Fadil, and the leading circles of the city."

Maimonides would never accept compensation for Torah study or discharging his rabbinic responsibilities as the principal authority in Egypt on Jewish law, in accordance with Talmudic rulings prohibiting receipt of emoluments from Torah study. His younger brother, David, supported the clan as an international merchant in the lucrative international trade until he drowned in the Indian Ocean while on a business trip to India in 1176–77. Moses, his older brother, was left responsible for David's widow and daughter and had to take up the practice of medicine to support the family. Maimonides fell into a debilitating depression over his loss. In a personal message he sent to Japheth ben Elijah, the judge, his former host in Acre, Moses detailed the psychic distress and physical pain he suffered when his brother drowned: "The worst disaster that struck me of late, worse than anything I had ever experienced from the time I was born until this day, was the demise of that upright man, may the memory of the righteous be a blessing, who drowned in the Indian sea.... For about a year from the day the evil tidings reached me I remained dangerously ill with severe inflammation, fever, and numbness of heart, and well-nigh perished. From then until this day, that is, about eight years, I have been in a state of inconsolate mourning.... For he was my son; he grew up on my knees; he was my brother, my pupil. It was he who did business in the market place, earning a living while I dwelled in security. He had a quick grasp of Talmud and a superb mastery of grammar. My only joy was to see him. 'The sun has set on all joy' [Isa. 24:11]. For he has gone on to eternal life, leaving me dismayed on a foreign land [cf. the biblical Moses in Exod. 2:22, 18:3]. Whenever I see his handwriting or one of his books, my heart is churned inside me and my sorrow is rekindled. In short, 'I will go down mourning to my son in Sheol' [Gen. 37:35]."

A despondent Maimonides nevertheless preoccupied himself with completing his rabbinical magnum opus, the fourteen-volume *Mishneh Torah (Repetition of the Torah*, referring to Deut. 17:18) known in English as *The Code of Jewish Law*. Maimonides referred to the work in Arabic as *ta'lifuna al-kabir*, "my great Composition," and in Hebrew as *ha-Hibbur*, "The Compilation." It also came to be known as *Yad ha-hazaqa*, "The Mighty Hand," because the numerical value of the two letters of the Hebrew word for "hand," "yod" (ten) + "dalet" (four), equal fourteen. Written in his own beautifully rendered register of rabbinic Hebrew, Moses completed the work around 1178. This monumental, systematic compendium of Jewish law (*halakha*) aimed to make *halakha* uniform and render it accessible to all who lacked the expertise to ascertain the law through study of the intricate, dialectical Talmudic debates and subsequent Geonic and post-geonic rulings. The *Mishneh Torah* drew on and fulfilled the plan, first suggested in the *Commentary on the Mishnah* and subsequently in the *Book of Commandments*, to organize and standardize all of Jewish law, biblical and rabbinic, the Written Torah and the Oral Torah: "I have seen fit to divide this compilation by laws according to topic; and I shall divide the laws into chapters according to that topic; and each and every chapter I shall divide into smaller laws so that they might be committed to memory."

The *Mishneh Torah* also selectively incorporated theological principles and codified them as incumbent on every Jew to uphold. This assertive doctrinal turn was unprecedented in rabbinic legal tradition in its ambition. In addition to delineating the totality of divine law without recourse to its post-biblical sources or dissenting opinions, Maimonides called upon his religious community to love God with their minds. It was a novel, bold, and challenging move aimed at combating what Maimonides construed as rampant popular forms of idolatry and superstition. *The Code*'s form and substance proved to be controversial and provoked opposition in certain quarters, especially in northern Spain and France.

Following publication of *The Code*, Maimonides' reputation grew apace to legendary status. His standing as a singularly respected rabbinic authority is reflected in the voluminous legal queries he received from individuals near and far. They were recorded and disseminated in the literary form of *responsa* (legal opinions), nearly five hundred of which have survived in printed editions and Geniza manuscripts. Maimonides also engaged in more extended formal correspondence as in the *Epistle to Yemen*; with the *Treatise on Resurrection* (1190–91), an epistolary essay clarifying his views on resurrection of the dead in response to allegations Samuel ben 'Eli, head of the rabbinical academy in Baghdad, leveled against him; with the rabbis of Provence over contemporary disputes such as the legal status of astrology (*Letter on Astrology*, 1194), as well as in occasional letters to individuals concerning personal issues or to communities involving doctrinal matters (*Letter to Joseph ben Judah, Letter to Obadiah the*

Proselyte, Letter to Hasdai Halevi, Letter to Joseph ibn Jabir, Letter to the Sages of Lunel).

Despite his burdensome medical, communal, and rabbinic responsibilities, and the birth of his beloved son Abraham in 1186 when he was already forty-seven years old, Maimonides spent five years working on *The Guide of the Perplexed*. The work is formally addressed to his protege, Joseph ben Judah ibn Simon, and like-minded Jewish intellectual elites and capable others confounded by the relationship between Torah, science, and philosophy. *The Guide* is a magisterial study of the complementary roles of reason and revelation in religious life and particularly the problem of anthropomorphic language and the physical and metaphysical secrets inscribed in the Hebrew Bible. Even more than the *Mishneh Torah* (which in theory rendered unnecessary advanced Talmudic study and dispensed with citing sources in accordance with traditional practice), *The Guide* generated as much controversy as adulation because of suspicions that it departed radically from traditional and popular Jewish beliefs. When Samuel ibn Tibbon, the *Guide*'s Hebrew translator in Provence, requested a meeting with him in 1199 to consult over some difficult passages, Maimonides, sixty-one at the time, memorably described the draining weekday routine that made any such visit completely out of the question.

In the 1190s Maimonides began to compose *consilia*—short medical works devoted to treating specific ailments—at the request of Muslim dignitaries. *On the Regimen of Health* and *On the Elucidation of Some Symptoms and the Response to Them* were written for the Egyptian ruler al-Malik al-Afdal 'Ali, Saladin's eldest son, who suffered from constipation, indigestion, and depression. Maimonides drafted *On Coitus* for an unidentified notable anxious to maintain and enhance his virility. According to his own testimony it seems that only Maimonides' increasingly irregular opportunities for solitude, study, and contemplation and his deep love for his son, Abraham, sustained him in his final years.

He confessed as much to Joseph ben Judah ibn Simon: "When I consider the condition of this world, I find consolation only in two things: in contemplating and studying and in my son Abraham, for God (the exalted) has given him grace and blessing of his namesake...he is humble and has fine moral qualities, and he has a subtle mind and fine nature. And with the help of God he shall no doubt have a name among the great [cf. 1 Chron. 17:8]."

What can we glean about Maimonides' frame of mind during the final years of his life? His letters return time and again to his burdens, his infirmity, and his profound concern for the survival of advanced Torah study informed by science and philosophy. The twelfth century was marked by eschatological and millenarian expectation among Muslims, Christians, and Jews alike. The Crusades and the exchange of control over Jerusalem from Christian to Islamic rule and the multiple tribulations the Jews experienced during the twelfth century certainly exacerbated his people's longing for their ultimate deliverance from exile, increased their speculation about the advent of the messianic era, and even engendered activity to hasten its arrival. Maimonides' perspective on the persona of the Messiah, the timing of the messianic age, and his halakhic exposition of its naturalistic character were highly debated matters. They remain contested questions in Maimonidean studies alongside arguments about his perspective on the legitimacy of poetry, his misogyny, and his closely held views on the resurrection of the dead.

Some of Maimonides' Provencal followers seem to have taken his singular achievements and unique standing among the Jews as a sign of the imminent coming of the Messiah. A lengthy rhymed prose Hebrew letter in 1195/96 to Maimonides from Jonathan ha-Kohen, head of the Lunel rabbinical academy, requests his expert assistance in grappling with certain difficult passages in *The Guide*. The epistle deploys soaring rhetoric and multiple biblical allusions to Maimonides' modesty, leadership, learning, and godliness. It represents Moses as comparable to his biblical namesake, unrivaled as the ultimate prophet of Israel as the giver of Torah. The epistle's reference to Isaiah 63:11 ("Then he remembered the ancient days, Him, who pulled his people [*mosheh*] out [of the water]") also connects Moses and Moses ben Maimon to divine redemption: "Isn't he called by the name 'Moses'? He extricates (Heb. *mosheh*) his people from the waters of error recalling days of yore...to strengthen the covenant of the Patriarchs, the covenant of Horeb and Sinai, to instruct the Children of Israel the ordinances the Lord commanded." Jonathan's letter and various Geniza documents construe Maimonides as a singularly foundational Jewish figure and wishfully as the "second Moses" who prefigures the imminent appearance of the Messiah. On the basis of contemporary sources lionizing him (e.g., "the Moses of his generation," "Moses, my Servant" [Num. 12:7]; "Moses, the man of God" [Deut. 33:1]), Maimonides' reply in kind to Jonathan's letter, various cryptic statements in his writings concerning the attainment of prophecy, his father's encouragement in naming him, and the tradition regarding "Moses redivivus," Abraham Joshua Heschel among his modern readers even wondered whether Maimonides thought that he had attained prophecy and accordingly viewed himself as a harbinger of the messianic age. What is certain is that for Maimonides, the Messiah's arrival was conditional upon the restoration of prophecy and the appearance of a prophet to prepare the way for his rule.

Maimonides died in Cairo in 1204 at the age of sixty-six. According to tradition, he was buried in Tiberias (Ayyubid Palestine) in accordance with his wishes. His son, Abraham Maimonides, succeeded him as recognized head of the Egyptian Jewish community and followed in his footsteps as a physician, learned rabbinic authority, and profound religious thinker. He also committed himself to serve as the guardian of his father's incomparable legacy. Abraham devoted three treatises to preserving and defending that inheritance. Among Moses' acolytes during his lifetime and immediately thereafter, Judah al-Harizi, stands out as an articulate voice for Maimonides' otherworldly sway touching every dimension of Jewish life in Islamdom and his role in consummating Andalusi Jewish tradition and culture. Al-Harizi translated the *Epistle on Resurrection*, *The Guide of the Perplexed*, and part of the *Commentary on the Mishnah* from Arabic to Hebrew for "the sages and nobles" of Provence. Al-Harizi was a Hebrew and Arabic belletrist from Toledo who journeyed from Iberia via Provence to the Islamic East, shortly after the turn of the thirteenth century, where he met Abraham Maimonides. He paid extraordinary tribute to Abraham in the *Tahkemoni*, his collection of Hebrew rhymed prose *maqamat* (rhetorical anecdotes) and in the Arabic *Kitab al-durar* (*The Book of Pearls: In Praise of Communities*), the most "objective" of three "accounts" (the other two more literary and imaginative) of the author's travels in the East. Defending Moses against his enemies, al-Harizi extols him in praise bordering on veneration, even accounting for the conventions of poetic hyperbole:

A mortal of the divine saints and elect of God who was the paragon of his generation, of Law and faith, the light. Prodigy of the sphere and sovereign of the heights, diadem of nobility and the nations' light, our teacher Moses son of Maymun.... For he had enlightened the darkness of ignorant hearts, and through his science slumbering souls awakened, healing through his intelligence, the feeble minds, and rectifying through his judgment corrupt beliefs. He illumined the eyes through his compositions which were a guide for the perplexed, and bestowing perfection upon the unaccomplished, he endeared repentance unto the unbelievers.... Verily he was of the unique individuals among the saints, whose rank drew near to that of prophets....

...and the Lord reared for his nation, this master Moses, may God be pleased with him, who codified the judicial subjects and religious traditions, abridging their length without omission. He assembled all their principles, arranged all their details, levelled their asperity, revealed their mysteries, so that the legal sciences, and religious regulations, became fluent to their lips, and easy and plain to their seeker, and flowed like honey upon the tongue. Their meaning was not arduous for readers, and those possessed of intelligence were no longer in need of a master to mediate it. He revived intelligence after its death and restored the disappearing Torah after it had elapsed. Through his books the ignorant became scholars, and the foolish became men of understanding. It has become clear to you from my words that the substance of Divine providence, and the effusion of the prophetic faculty had unceasingly flowed from Ezra the leader, up till this master Moses.

Chapter 2
"Back home in the west"

Like many Andalusi Muslim and Jewish intellectuals, Moses Maimonides expressed immense pride in his place of origin. He continued to identify himself as a Jew of Sefarad long after he left al-Andalus and established permanent roots in Egypt. His earliest major composition, the *Commentary on the Mishnah* (completed in 1168), opens with the declaration: "I am Moses ben Maimon, the Sephardi." A slightly more elaborate formula is reiterated in the *Letter on Astrology* dated 1194; and the *Letter to Yemen* (1172) commences with the assertion, "I am one of the least of the sages of Sefarad whose adornment has been stripped by Exile." Maimonides also utilized the Arabic phrases *'indana fi l-andalus, 'indana fi l-maghrib*, and their variants, literally "at our place in al-Andalus" or "at our place in the West (North Africa and al-Andalus)," but more idiomatically "back home in al-Andalus/ the West" or "by us in al-Andalus/the West" to identify Arabic idioms distinctive to al-Andalus, and Andalusi scientific and philosophical traditions. He employed the same catchphrase to label rabbinic interpretations, rulings, customs, and practices specific to the Sephardi Jewish heritage in which he was reared and which he championed.

The acclaimed rabbinic scholar, philosopher, communal leader, and physician in Egypt, his adopted home, never ceased referring to his Sephardi origins or expressing effusive admiration for

Andalusi Jewish traditions and veneration for his teachers in the West. Maimonides' steadfast dedication to Andalusi learning transcended parochially Jewish subjects. It extended to astronomy, medicine, and philosophy. Maimonides thus singled out for approval Andalusi Jewish thinkers and Andalusi Muslim mathematicians, scientists, and philosophers in *Guide of the Perplexed* (ca. 1185–91), his exegetical-theological-philosophical masterpiece: "As for the Andalusians among the people of our nation, all of them cling to the affirmations of the philosophers and incline to their opinions, insofar as these do not ruin the foundation of the Law.... Then came latter day groups of people in Andalusia who became very proficient in mathematics and explained, conforming to Ptolemy's premises, that Venus and Mercury were above the sun. In fact, Ibn al-Aflah of Sevillia, whose son I have met, has written a celebrated book about this. Thereupon, the excellent philosopher Abu Bakr Ibn al-Sa'igh, under the guidance of one of whose pupils I have read texts, reflected on this notion and showed various ways of argumentation...." As for medicine, Maimonides' *Glossary on Pharmaceuticals* and his respect for North African physicians evince his Andalusi-Maghribi education and experiences in that elect professional sphere.

What exactly was the Andalusi Jewish cultural inheritance in which Maimonides was immersed during his formative years? The heritage that defined much of his life's work turned on the complete Arabization of the Jews of Islamdom west of Iran. Jewish intellectuals' skill in reading literary Arabic, the common language of erudition in Islamdom, served them as an indispensable tool in Islamic society. It opened for them a new universe whose powers they employed in adapting Jewish tradition and cultural production to life in "Islamicate" society and civilization, the term that scholars now use to accommodate the presence and participation of Christians, Jews, and Zoroastrians in classical Islamdom. To put it another way, Jewish writers and thinkers absorbed and appropriated Arabo-Islamic learning and found inventive ways to apply it to their understanding of Jewish tradition, thought, and practice.

The transformation of Jewish intellectual and cultural life that Arabizing wrought began during the ninth century in the Islamic East and was conveyed to al-Andalus via the regional centers of Jewish learning in Kairouan and Fez in North Africa. In al-Andalus Jewish scholarly and literary production reached its fullest expression beginning in the tenth century, a two-centuries-long period known as the "Golden Age of the Jews in Spain." Well before Maimonides, Andalusi Jewish religious and literary intellectuals devoted themselves to the same disciplines and arts Muslim scholars and literati employed in Qur'anic study and its related branches of Arabic language and Islamic learning, law, and lore. For Jewish scholars, the curriculum comprised linguistic analysis of the lexicon and grammar of biblical Hebrew, rational and aesthetic exegesis of the Hebrew Bible, reason-based theology and philosophy, and the development of new literary genres dedicated to the systematic inquiry and organization of rabbinic law. Before the mid-twelfth century all their inquiries were conducted in the Arabic language. They reserved Hebrew for ceremonial purposes, elevated rhymed prose introductions, formal communications, and especially for liturgical and social poetry.

Following the practice of Andalusi Jewish scholars until the mid-twelfth century, Maimonides composed all but one of his major works—that is, those devoted to Jewish subjects for a strictly Jewish readership—in Arabic, his mother tongue. To be more precise, Maimonides' written Arabic was a literary register of Judeo-Arabic, the Jewish dialect of Middle Arabic that served as the vernacular for all Islamdom's residents west of Iran. Written Judeo-Arabic was represented in Hebrew characters interspersed with Hebrew idioms and textual references to Jewish life and tradition. Judeo-Arabic served as Maimonides' literary language from the *Commentary on the Mishnah* (1161–68), his early, first literary statement of rabbinic law, to various occasional letters, epistles, and treatises replying to individual concerns or communal issues directed to him such as the *Epistle to Yemen* regarding persecution and the appearance of a false messiah, the *Treatise on Resurrection* (ca. 1191) defending his views on the meaning of the rabbinic doctrine "resurrection of the dead," *The Guide of the Perplexed*, and many of his rabbinic *responsa* addressing legal queries he received from near and far.

For his philosophical and scientific works written for a general and not expressly Jewish audience such as the *Treatise on the Art of Logic* (ca. 1160) and his corpus of medical writings, Maimonides' Arabic approximated the classical language. In such instances, it is possible he employed Arabic script rather than the Hebrew characters utilized in Jewish texts or perhaps copyists transcribed such works into Arabic letters for their wider readership. By contrast, Maimonides composed the *Mishneh Torah*, his rabbinic summa that is a compendium of Jewish law in its entirety, in an unrivaled self-designed register of rabbinic Hebrew to make it accessible to Jews in communities beyond Arabic-speaking lands. He cites an additional literary consideration for his choice of language in the work's introduction: the *Mishneh Torah* was composed "in clear language and succinctly so that the whole of the Oral Law might be set forth for all. [All this while] leaving aside argument and counterargument...[limiting the exposition to] clear, plausible, juridically correct things...."

Ibn 'Aqnin (Maimonides' countryman and probable acquaintance in Fez) outlined the parameters of Andalusi Judeo-Arabic education in a highly structured program for advanced Jewish and scientific studies. Following Andalusi Aristotelian tradition, Ibn 'Aqnin's *Hygiene of the Soul* set forth a curriculum leading the aspiring young intellectual through a staged sequence of subjects and disciplines, from reading and writing to expressly Jewish subjects: Torah, Mishnah, Hebrew grammar, poetry (on religious themes), and Talmud, followed by more general philosophical observations on religion, philosophic studies, logic, mathematics, optics, astronomy, music, mechanics, natural sciences, and medicine, culminating in metaphysics. Viewed another way, Ibn 'Aqnin's prospectus engages three intersecting lines of inquiry and cultural production that marked the Andalusi Jewish Arabizing subculture in which Maimonides was steeped: defining Hebrew linguistic eloquence and cultivating Hebrew aesthetic refinement; scientific query, empiricism, and rationalism in the quest for wisdom and enlightenment; and analytic rigor in rabbinic research, systematization of religious law, and enacting uniformity of practice. The Aristotelian philosopher and chronicler Abraham ibn Daud, Maimonides' older contemporary who fled Almohad al-Andalus for Toledo in Christian Castile, put it more succinctly in *The Book of Tradition*: Andalusi scholars were distinguished by a common intellectual tradition combining Torah, "Greek wisdom" (i.e., science and philosophy as transmitted in Arabic), and Hebrew letters. Maimonides mastered these specialized spheres and methods of Andalusi learning and each figures prominently in his written works. Indeed, he represents the culmination of this process of integrating Arabo-Islamic learning in every domain of Andalusi Jewish cultural production except for Hebrew poetry.

Hebrew eloquence

Arabized Hebrew and Judeo-Arabic literature embody the Jewish adaptation of Arabo-Islamic practices, thought, and values—the nexus of which is called *adab* in Arabic. In its most capacious sense, *adab* signifies erudition, sophisticated culture, and etiquette. More narrowly, it connotes literature and literary creativity. The Andalusi Jews' *adab* revolved completely around their Arabization and the ways in which it inspired their appreciation of the classical Hebrew language, its aesthetic virtues and artistic capacity. The Andalusi Jewish literary and religious intellectuals' determination to revive Hebrew from what they deemed its lamented, historically long neglect and forgotten status in the lands of exile was preceded by scholars in the Islamic East during the late ninth and tenth centuries. The most prominent rabbanite intellectual of his time and place, Sa'adia Gaon, in effect "converted" a critical Islamic doctrine regarding the "inimitable" language and style of the Qur'an into a principle of Hebrew aesthetics: Sa'adia aspired to uncover and reproduce the "eloquent clarity" of biblical Hebrew. This fresh approach to the Hebrew Bible taken up by Sa'adia and his successor, Samuel ben Hofni Gaon, also drew upon models of Quranic exegesis to create a new approach to biblical interpretation. Henceforth Judeo-Arabic biblical exegesis combined philology, grammar, and a refined literary sensibility along with science, philosophy, and in matters of *halakha*, traditional rabbinic understanding. It thus assumed that the true meaning of the Hebrew Bible could not deviate from reason, science, or rabbinic legal rulings, respectively. Scholars set about demonstrating the veracity of this assumption using the "linguistic sciences" and all the newly available intellectual, literary, and philological tools at their disposal.

Arabized Jewish intellectuals in al-Andalus, religious and literary alike, endeavored to decrypt, define, and ultimately revive eloquent classical Hebrew style. On the heels of Sa'adia Gaon's and the Karaities' undertakings in the East, North African and Andalusi Jewish comparative philologians "discovered" the deep linguistic affinities between Arabic, Hebrew, and Aramaic and then applied their knowledge to biblical lexicography and exegesis. Renowned philologists such as Judah Hayyuj and Jonah ibn Janah, the pre-eminent lexicographer and grammarian of biblical Hebrew, explained biblical Hebrew lexicography and grammar in accordance with Arabic linguistic paradigms. Ibn Janah asserted that "for Arabic after Aramaic is the language which most resembles ours." Many years later Maimonides put it somewhat differently: "and as for the Arabic and Hebrew languages, all who know them both agree they are one language without a doubt," an opinion he restated with a slight variation in his *Medical Aphorisms:* "Regarding the Arabic and Hebrew vernaculars, it is accepted by everyone who knows the two languages that they are undoubtedly a single language and Aramaic is very closely related to them...."

Biblical exegetes, many of whom were linguistic scholars themselves, put the new knowledge with its literal-minded linguistic, rational, and context-based interpretive methods to use in biblical commentaries mirroring the work of their earlier Muslim counterparts in Quranic studies. For their part, such eminent Hebrew poets as Samuel the Nagid and Moses ibn 'Ezra and thinker-poets Solomon ibn Gabirol and Judah Halevi composed exquisite liturgical and Arabic-style social poetry and elevated rhymed prose in accordance with Sa'adia's idealization of Hebrew "words beautifully put." By Maimonides' time, the body of Andalusi Jewish Judeo-Arabic linguistic research, biblical exegesis, poetics, and Hebrew lyrics was extensive and widely disseminated among the Jewish communities of Islamdom.

Maimonides' expert knowledge of biblical Hebrew owed much to his predecessors' systematic philological and grammatical inquiries and Judeo-Arabic poetics. He also absorbed the Andalusi Jewish rational, historical-contextual, and literary-aesthetic methods of biblical exegesis and applied them in his discriminating reading of Scripture. Maimonides however never presented his scriptural exegesis in the form of a running biblical commentary or offered his philological conclusions in a discrete lexicographical work: the reader must glean his innumerable lexicographical comments, biblical explanations, and interpretive principles from the scriptural citations in his writings across the genres. Maimonides' keen attention to the language of the Hebrew Bible in *The Guide* was informed by the preoccupation with figurative and metaphorical language in Andalusi Hebrew and Judeo-Arabic poetics and his understanding of the power of language and its limitations, especially when addressing the nature of God. *The Guide*'s introduction and first chapters contend with what Maimonides deems "equivocal terms and parables": "The first purpose of this Treatise is to explain the meanings of certain terms occurring in the books of prophecy.... This Treatise also has a second purpose: namely the explanation of very obscure parables occurring in the books of the prophets, but not explicitly identified there as such."

Above all Maimonides was deeply concerned with the prevalence of literal readings of the Hebrew Bible's numerous anthropomorphic figures of speech pertaining to God and God's "actions." His insistent avowal of *tawhid*, God's absolute unity, requires figurative understanding of biblical representations of God and affirmation of divine incorporeality, including the denial of divine attributes. Andalusi scholars like Maimonides enjoyed relatively wide latitude in explaining biblical narrative, poetry, and material of a theological nature. Andalusi Jewish rationalists were far more circumscribed in interpreting passages from the Torah of a legal nature (which did not elicit a figurative interpretation) because of the authority of rabbinic tradition and their fidelity to it.

Maimonides' rhymed prose letters, ornate Hebrew introductions to Arabic works intended for a Jewish audience, and even a few short poetic preambles identify him as a masterful Andalusi Hebrew stylist even if he was not a poet. Consider the conclusion of the flowery and playfully allusive rhymed prose introduction to one of a cluster of communications in the late 1190s with Jonathan ben David ha-Cohen (the head of the rabbinic academy) and the sages of Lunel regarding their queries on the *Mishneh Torah*. Maimonides confessed that he composed the opening passages of his letter in ornate rhymed Hebrew prose because poetic language is "the manner of our fellows in the past, to which all of our brothers in Sefarad turned." Above all, the most compelling signs of Maimonides' appreciation for Andalusi Hebrew aesthetics, albeit with Maimonidean twists, is the uniquely exquisite and elegant style of rabbinic Hebrew he fashioned for the *Mishneh Torah* and his (Neoplatonic) vision of God's absolute, transcendent goodness and beauty. Bolstering his Andalusi predecessors' and Sa'adia Gaon's ideological commitment to Hebrew, Maimonides repeated a rabbinic source reckoning study of the "holy tongue" among the divine commandments (although he did not count it as such in his *Book of Commandments*).

Like his Andalusi predecessors and Sa'adia Gaon, Maimonides appreciated the purity, clarity, and stylistic beauty of biblical Hebrew. Yet he expanded the historical register of pristine Hebrew by regarding its rabbinic phase, evidenced in language of the *Mishnah*, as an ideal iteration of its linguistic virtue. Because of his intellectually ambitious projects and the diverse audiences he addressed in his writings, Maimonides valued the exacting use of precise language as an instrument of effective communication and pedagogy. He also embraced the Andalusi Jewish devotion to stylistic elegance as valuable so long as it served to enhance conveying Torah and wisdom in the *Mishneh Torah*, what the historian of Jewish law Isadore Twersky deemed "the successful fusion of content and form." Joseph ibn Jabir, one of Maimonides' enthusiasts in Baghdad, studied the Arabic *Commentary on the Mishnah* and *Book of the Commandments*. He wrote to Maimonides asking if he would translate the *Mishneh Torah* into Arabic. Maimonides responded by gently encouraging his devoted follower to study Hebrew. He would not translate the *Mishneh Torah* into Arabic since "I composed *The Code* in it [Hebrew] because it is easy to understand and quite straightforward to master." Maimonides also expressed occasional regret that he had written certain works in Arabic and had to leave their translation into Hebrew to other scholars.

Maimonides' views on language in general and especially Hebrew departed in complex ways from those of his predecessors. He adhered to Aristotle and the pre-eminent Muslim philosophers of the Islamic East who followed him, al-Farabi and Ibn Sina (Avicenna), along with Sa'adia Gaon and Abraham ibn 'Ezra, in holding that languages, including Hebrew, originate by human convention, not by nature or through any metaphysical impetus.

By contrast, another strata of Sa'adia's work (and that of Abraham ibn 'Ezra in his own manner) embraced the traditional rabbinic valorization of Hebrew as primordial, divine, and thus exceptional among languages, a perspective Judah Halevi asserted even more emphatically as an adaptation of the incomparable status of Quranic Arabic in Islam. Most Andalusi Jewish scholars before Maimonides equivocated between the conventional and revelational perspectives. For his part Maimonides recognized the singular nobility of Hebrew as *lᵉshon ha-qodesh* in the sense of "the language of the sacred" rather than in its commonplace gist as "the Holy Tongue." He considered the relative absence of sexual and execratory expressions and vulgar terms in Hebrew to constitute its unique distinction. At the same time Maimonides' comments on Galen's avowal of the superiority of Greek over other languages draws upon al-Farabi to assert that all the languages spoken by people living in temperate climes, including Hebrew, Arabic, Persian, Aramaic, and Greek, are the most pleasant.

Pursuit of wisdom and truth

Before Maimonides, the intellectual transformation of Jewish culture in classical Islamdom, alongside the conjunction of Arabic and Hebrew in linguistics, biblical exegesis, and literary artistry, also turned on the intersection of Jewish tradition and the revival in Islamic civilization of Greek science, rationalism, and the proclivity to think systematically and organize what is learned and known. The Andalusi Jewish quest for wisdom, like the cultivation of linguistic eloquence, drew upon foundational developments in intellectual life going back several centuries in the Islamic East and Abbasid Baghdad. There and then Muslims encountered the scientific and philosophical traditions of ancient Greece that had been preserved in Christian Syriac translations. The political leaders of Islamdom undoubtedly deemed this knowledge, especially mathematics, astronomy, and natural science, including medicine, indispensable in the consolidation, strengthening, and administration of empire. Accordingly, the Abbasid caliph Harun al-Rashid (r. 786–809), who appears as an idealized figure in the *Thousand and One Nights*, and his son and successor, al-Ma'mun (r. 813–33), were assumed to be patrons of the budding arts and sciences in Islamic civilization. What came to be called the "translation movement" was driven primarily by the intellectual curiosity of urban Muslim intellectual elites. In due course the Christian Syriac versions of Greek texts were rendered into Arabic. Since these texts did not appear to encroach directly on Islamic practice or belief, even Muslim religious scholars found their learning could be valuable in determining practical matters such as the precise orientation of Mecca for the construction of mosques.

The universal, humanistic components of Greek thought, especially Aristotle's writings, formed the core of the scientific and philosophical translations into Arabic. This corpus quickly penetrated the circles of court secretaries, viziers, literati, and religious intellectuals focused on the articulation and understanding of Islam itself in the guise of rational theology. Initially for polemical purposes, rabbanite and Karaite intellectuals along with Levantine Christians responded to the cultural moment by engaging the same material in Arabic. They applied its methods, concepts, and idioms to probing and demonstrating the rational footing of their own scripture and subsequent religious tradition. The pursuit of intellectual enlightenment thus became a predominant force in Islamic civilization for each of its confessional communities.

Maimonides' work as philosopher of religion was preceded by two centuries of Jewish religious philosophy under Islam, when systematic thinking became a religious obligation for Muslim, Christian, and Jewish intellectual elites. *Kalam* (literally "word") was the Arabic term used to signify "rational theology." *'Ilm al-kalam* ("science of the word," that is rational theology) was not philosophy, but as practiced by the *mutakallimun* (practitioners of rational theology) an apologetic and defensive discourse ("orderly expression") utilizing philosophical methods to demonstrate the metaphysical truths of revelation and religious tradition. Among the earliest schools of Islamic thought the Mu'tazila (fl. mid-eighth to tenth century; literally, "those who withdraw" but applied to "those who uphold an intermediate position" on the question of whether a severe sinner is a Muslim or an apostate) were known as *ahl al-tawhid wa-l-'adl*. These "advocates of (God's) Oneness and Justice," privileged God's absolute divine unity and probity in dispensing reward and punishment among the most significant things that could be said and known about God. They were displaced by orthodox schools of Islamic thought and relegated to heretical status because their avowal of human free will appeared to diminish God's foreknowledge and causation of everything.

Mu'tazilite *kalam* and its Ash'arite (the most important Sunni school of Islamic theology) adaptation as well as their new approach to what could be predicated of God, that is, the divine attributes, appealed to Jewish thinkers like Sa'adia Gaon who reworked it for their own purposes.

Sa'adia's *Book of Beliefs and Opinions* represents a systematic defense of rabbinic Judaism using the critical tools and concepts the Mu'tazila developed along with incorporating Neoplatonic and Aristotelian elements of thought. To be more specific, Sa'adia's epistemology and cosmology endeavored to demonstrate, that is, to prove the empirical and rational basis for the Hebrew Bible, rabbinic law, and doctrines such as the Creator's existence and unity, and *creatio ex nihilo* ("creation out of nothing") in response to various challenges to rabbanite tradition.

Sa'adia's North African contemporaries and successors and the earliest Andalusi thinkers such as Solomon ibn Gabirol (Avicebron; *The Font of Life*), the pietist Bahya ibn Paquda (*Book of Direction to the Duties of the Heart*), and Judah Halevi (*The Kuzari/The Book of Refutation and Proof on the Despised Faith*) were Neoplatonists each after his own particular fashion.

39

Neoplatonism arrived in al-Andalus through multiple channels. The North African physician and philosopher Isaac ben Solomon Israeli and his student Dunash ben Tamim seem to have introduced Neoplatonism to Jewish thought and, along with Sa'adia's writings, were principal Jewish conduits for Andalusi Jewish religious thought in the eleventh century. So, too, the works of eastern Muslim thinkers such as al-Kindi, the first philosopher to write in Arabic, and the *Rasa'il ikhwan al-safa'* (*Epistles of the Pure Brethren*), an anonymous encyclopedic collection of Neoplatonic writings devoted to the contemporary sciences and the quest for truth, appear to have made their way to al-Andalus by the mid-tenth century. The Neoplatonic mystic Ibn Masarrah was the first Muslim figure of consequence in the history of Andalusi thought. With its emphasis on the notion of the soul's longing to reunite with its ethereal Source, Neoplatonism dominated Jewish religious thought in al-Andalus until shortly before Maimonides.

Maimonides utterly disdained *kalam* on account of its assumptions, inconsistencies, and philosophical limitations. Accordingly, he was critical of the *mutakallimun* as well as Neoplatonic authors whose writings he encountered in Fatimid Egypt even if, like other philosophers, he incorporated Neoplatonic elements into his work. Maimonides' new home was marked by its distinctive Isma'ili theological orientation and its rationalism, esotericism, and humanistic inclination. Like their North African-Andalusi rivals the Almohads, the Isma'ilis stressed *tawhid* and denied anthropomorphic representations (*tashbih*) of God. Accordingly, Isma'ili thought developed its own metaphorical Quranic exegesis (*ta'wil*), stressing the limitations of human language in describing God and, in particular, adopting the doctrine of "negative divine attributes."

Maimonides affords us a glimpse of his philosophical library in his missive (1199) to Samuel ibn Tibbon in Provence regarding the latter's problems in translating *The Guide of the Perplexed* into Hebrew from Arabic and his futile request to consult with Maimonides in person. Maimonides' letter indicates the master's staunch dedication to philosophy over rational theology. It concludes with Maimonides' recommended syllabus for Samuel, the serious student of philosophy. To comprehend correctly the philosophical principles informing *The Guide*, Maimonides urges Samuel to read and study Aristotle along with the commentaries of Alexander of Aphrodisias and Themistius, as well as that of Ibn Rushd (whose work Maimonides likely read only after completing *The Guide*). Among the roster of latter-day philosophers, al-Farabi ("all of his writings are excellent") and the Andalusi Ibn Bajja ("[he] was a great philosopher, and all of his writings are of a high standard") garner Maimonides' enthusiastic endorsements. By contrast, he downplayed the importance of Ibn Sina, the renowned Persian philosopher, probably on account of the latter's decidedly Neoplatonic thrust. Be that as it may, for Maimonides Aristotle surpasses them all, once divested of pagan, naturalistic ideas contrary to the notion of "creation out of nothing" and God's uncaused, eternal and unique Oneness: "The books of Aristotle are the roots and foundations of all the works on the sciences.... Aristotle reached the utmost limit of knowledge which one can achieve, unless the divine emanation is bestowed upon him so that he attains the stage of prophecy above which there is no higher stage."

Notwithstanding the Almohads' treatment of religious others and the issue of the Maimon clan's crypto-Judaism, Maimonides encountered Almohad thinking during his formative years in al-Andalus and Fez from 1148 to 1165. Recent research reveals his affinity for Almohad structures of thought and the ways in which his subsequent philosophical and legal works deeply engaged Almohad era models. The Almohad movement of revivalist Berbers (Ar. al-Muwahhidun; "those who proclaim God's absolute Oneness") emphasized a rational approach to the doctrine of Divine Unity and imposed upon everyone a non-anthropomorphic understanding of the Qur'an regardless of intellectual capacity and education. The "Almohad Creed" (*al-'Aqida*; 1183) was drafted by a court intellectual for the knowledgeable elite and presumably communicated by preachers to the multitude in filtered form. It stipulates a series of philosophical tenets about God based on deductive reasoning and drawn largely from Aristotle's *Metaphysics*, citations from the Qur'an, the *hadith* (canonical reports of the Prophet Muhammad's words and deeds), and Islamic law. Chapter 2 begins with its core methodological principle, "It is by the necessity of reason that the existence of God, praise to Him, is known," while chapter 7 sets forth a critical definition of God's unique Oneness: "And to understand the denial of the similarity between Creator and created is to understand the absolute existence of the Creator, since everything that has a beginning, and end, delimitation, and specialization must also have an extension in space, mutability...and a creator....There is nothing like Him which can be used as a term of comparison...."

The Creed was promulgated by the Almohad dynasty of Islamic religious revivalists before it took written form. Its central stipulation of *tawhid* ("the absolute unity of God") was followed by the principles of God's incorporeality and eternality. Arabic chronicles report that Muhammad ibn Tumart, the revolutionary movement's founder and self-proclaimed *Mahdi* (conventionally, the "rightly guided" End Times figure in Sunni Islam), was incensed by the ignorance of or turning away from the primary tenets and sources of Islam among the community of Muslims, especially the rival Almoravids. He was determined to restore and enforce these theological and legal fundamentals. The ensuing "Almohad Creed" was inspired by the great Persian theologian al-Ghazali's reiteration of the Prophet Muhammad's classic instruction to "command right and forbid wrong" and thereby bring justice and unity to the world. "The Creed" also drew substantially on Aristotle's metaphysics. Maimonides' doctrinal statements in the *Commentary to the Mishnah* and those distributed in the form of laws in the "Book of Knowledge" of the

Mishneh Torah mirror essential elements of Almohad thought while Judaizing their content through illustrations from the Hebrew Bible.

Systematizing and standardizing Torah

Preserving, propagating, and refining (although without always admitting as much) sacred law and religious tradition in a religious age was the defining intellectual endeavor for the Jews of al-Andalus, as it was for their predecessors in the Islamic East and North Africa. In his first major rabbinical work, the *Commentary on the Mishnah*, Maimonides mentions his father, Maimon, Isaac al-Fasi, and Joseph ibn Migash as his principal sources of halakhic information and inspiration. In one of his responsa Maimonides cites the succession of Sephardi rabbinic authorities to which he was heir: Moses ben Hanokh, Hanokh ben Moses, Isaac ibn Ghiyath, Isaac ben Barukh al-Balia, Isaac al-Fasi, and Joseph ben Meir ibn Migash (R 2:576 [#310]). The Jewish sages of al-Andalus whom Maimonides revered were party to a significant recentering of rabbinic research going back to the tenth century when regional rabbinic academies in the Islamic West began to achieve a level of advanced Talmudic scholarship on a par with the historic institutions in the Islamic East led by the classical Geonim (heads of rabbinic academies) in Iraq and Palestine. Maimonides was not merely a passive recipient and transmitter of specific rabbinic rulings and halakhic interpretations he was taught or a dispatcher of *responsa* to halakhic queries he received from near and far. Rather he assumed a dynamic role in bringing historical trends to their logical conclusion by producing a comprehensive, systematically organized code of Jewish law.

A few compendia of culled Talmudic law and lore appeared during the post-Talmudic period, but until Saʻadia Gaon, the heads of the rabbinical academies in the Islamic East generally restricted their literary activity to homilies and *responsa*. In addition to contributing to *responsa* literature and seeking to standardize rabbinic liturgy with publication of a siddur (prayer book), Sa'adia devised a new rabbinic literary genre that would have far-reaching effects on the analysis, presentation, and dissemination of Jewish law: individually authored Judeo-Arabic hala<u>kh</u>ic monographs addressing discrete legal topics preceded by an introduction. In effect, the hala<u>kh</u>ic monograph represented the first step in a centuries-long process of replacing the unwieldly arrangement of the Talmud's monumental corpus with the condensed and systematic organization of sacred law. Monographs, commentaries on the Talmud, manuals, and codes would render *hala<u>kh</u>a* accessible to educated Jews less conversant than professional scholars in the Talmud's intricate and challenging dialectics and cumbersome associative organization. These literary developments fostered by rabbinic scholars paralleled the *mu<u>kh</u>tasar* ("abridgment") genre adopted by the Islamic legal schools to simplify study of the prescriptions and proscriptions of divine law. Subsequently, the prolific Samuel ben Hofni Gaon composed a constellation of monographs devoted to civil law, amounting to a quasi-codification of that legal sphere. Sa'adia and Samuel's adoption of the terminology and concepts of Islamic legal theory was even more significant than the literary forms in constructing the sources of Jewish law and issuing definitive rulings over the course of the ensuing centuries.

Leading rabbinic authorities in the regional centers Kairouan and Lucena followed suit. Nissim ben Jacob ibn Shahin, head of the Kairouan academy, wrote the first systematic commentary-paraphrase on the Talmud and a reference aid to Talmudic study. Hananel ben Hushiel produced a commentary on the Talmud. His illustrious student, Isaac al-Fasi, who left North Africa for al-Andalus, composed a Talmudic digest on civil, criminal, and ritual laws entitled the *Book of Laws* (*Sefer ha-hala<u>kh</u>ot*). Joseph ibn Migash, al-Fasi's student and successor as head of the Lucena academy, authored a Talmudic commentary with a focus on textual exposition and deriving legal rulings for practical application. Isaac ibn Ghiya<u>th</u>, a poet, exegete, and rabbinic scholar, composed a commentary on the Talmud (*Book of the Lamp*; Ar. *Kitab al-siraj*) and *Halakhot keᵉlulot* (*Collected Halakhot*), a compilation of prescriptive legal decisions. These literary innovations were vehicles for addressing a substantive methodological issue and two socioreligious needs—how to render the rules and regulations of holy law more accessible to outposts of the religious community deficient in rabbinic expertise and how to standardize and unify Jewish practices. From halakhic monographs to digests to codes, the idea was to dispense with the intellectually demanding Talmudic dialectic and dissenting opinions, and to emphasize specific legal decisions to be observed in practice. This approach provided crucially important applied knowledge for local judges to consult in their administration of justice.

The thrust of these literary efforts culminated in Maimonides' comprehensive codification of Jewish law in the *Mishneh Torah*. Its systematic organization, classification, streamlined presentation, and definitive legal decisions (without sources or dissenting opinions) in fourteen volumes encompass all aspects of Jewish life, including sacred rituals in abeyance ever since the destruction of the Jerusalem Temple in the first century CE: *Knowledge*, *Adoration* (blessings, prayers, circumcision), *Seasons* (sabbath and festivals), *Women* (marriage and divorce), *Holiness* (illicit sexual unions and forbidden foods), *Asseverations* (oaths and vows), *Agriculture* (soil cultivation, Sabbatical and Jubilee years), *Temple Service* (the sanctuary and public sacrifices), *Offerings* (sacrifices by individuals), *Ritual Purity*, *Damages* (torts), *Acquisition* (commercial law), *Civil Laws* (debts and claims), *Judges* (evidence, civil administration, war), each book with its own subdivisions. As Maimonides put it, he construed the *Mishneh Torah* as a religious restoration and reform, in effect, a necessary response to what he reckoned an unprecedented historical crisis: "Excessive troubles and distressful times press upon all now.... Hence those interpretations and responses and laws, which the Geonim compiled and saw to rendering obvious, have in our times become difficult. Only a few in number properly understand their meanings. The same holds true for the Talmud itself.... For they require a broad understanding, a wise soul, and a long time, after which one may gather from them what is the straight way as regards things forbidden and permitted and the rest of the laws of the Torah...." He therefore composed the work "so that all the laws might be evident to minor and adult alike...so that no man would ever have need of another compilation as regards any one of the laws of Israel. Rather this compilation will gather together the entire Oral Law."

Maimonides was well aware of the revolutionary nature of his effort and anticipated the resistance to it as he notes in a letter to his disciple Joseph ben Judah: "Know that I have not composed this compendium [the *Mishneh Torah*] to gain authority among the Jews or to achieve fame, so that I should be distressed by opposition to the aim for which I composed it. I have only composed it in the first place, God knows, for myself, to be released from study and searching for what is needed, as well as for the time of old age and for the sale of God.... For by God, 'I am moved by zeal for the Lord,' God of Israel [1 Kings 19:10, 14], as I have witnessed a community lacking in a true [legal] collection and without correct, precisely formulated opinions. I accordingly carried out what I did for the sake of God alone...."

Following in the footsteps of their Geonic forebears, Andalusi Jewish scholars strove to authenticate the epistemological foundations of Torah—Oral and Written—in a chain of transmission going back to Moses at Mt. Sinai. To put it another way, rabbanite epistemology insisted on the absolute divine origin of both the "roots," that is, the principles, and "branches," the details, of Jewish law. Maimonides appeared to agree with this traditional stance, since his eighth doctrinal principle stipulates: "Torah from Heaven. The entire Torah found in our hands this day is the Torah that was revealed to Moses, and all of it was from the Almighty, in what is called metaphorically 'speech.'" Nevertheless,

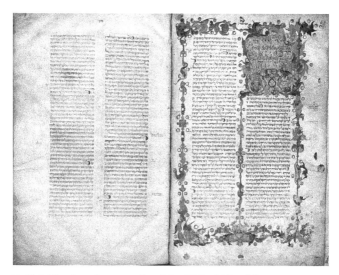

5. This illuminated manuscript of the *Mishneh Torah* from fifteenth-century Italy is a later medieval copy of Maimonides' magisterial *Code of Jewish Law*.

recent research has drawn attention to a more complex Maimonidean perspective on the active role Andalusi Jewish scholars living in a Maliki Islamic environment played in producing post-biblical law. According to this view, the "Oral Torah" revealed by God to Moses and transmitted to the sages down through the ages was somewhat more limited in scope. Generations of scholars thus contributed to the development of rabbinic law (within the parameters set by the Written and Oral Torah) through intellectual effort. Accordingly, the articulation of Jewish law was a process marked by continuity, modification, and innovation.

Maimonides' master plan to systematize and delineate the entirety of Jewish law for once and for all led him from the *Commentary on the Mishnah* to its companion volume, the *Book of the Commandments*, and the *Mishneh Torah*. In the introduction to the latter composition, he explains the architecture and relationship of these works and the unity of their purpose:

> After having completed our previous well-known work wherein we included a commentary to the whole Mishnah—our goal in that work having been satisfied with the explanation of the substance of each and every *halakhah* in the Mishnah, since our intention there was not to include an exhaustive discussion of the law of every commandment which would embrace all that is necessary (to know) of the prohibited and permissible, liable and free,... I deemed it advisable to compile a compendium which would include all of the laws of the Torah and its regulations, nothing missing in it. In this compendium I would try, as I am accustomed to do, to avoid mentioning differences of opinion and rejected teachings, and include in it only the established law, so that this compendium would embrace all the laws of the Torah of Moses our Teacher—whether they have bearing in the time of exile or not.... Similarly, I also found it advisable not to compose (this work) in the language of the Holy Scriptures, since that sacred language is too limited for us today to write the whole complex of the law in it.... I would compose it in the language of the Mishnah, so that it should be easily understood by most of the people. And I would include in it everything of the Torah that has been established and confirmed, omitting no question which might arise, or at least I would mention the principle by means of which that question can easily be resolved without too much deep reflection. Such was my goal to be in this work: brevity with completeness.... In short, outside of this work there was to be no need for another book to learn whatsoever that is required in the whole Torah, whether it be a law of the Scriptures or of the rabbis.

The Andalusi Jewish rabbinic heritage, itself the product of the interface of post-Talmudic tradition and the Islamic surroundings, thus served as a basis for Maimonides' lifelong project to fortify his community's accurate understanding and observance of Torah. The legal environment of Maimonides' youth inspired methodological, terminological, and practical aspects of his work on Jewish law just as its intellectual milieu stimulated Maimonides' religious thinking and informed his philosophy. His return to the fundamental sources of sacred law, his dismissal of the need to engage in or reproduce Talmudic lines of argumentation, his deletion of references to dissenting opinions and sources, and his inclusion of doctrinal principles all parallel Almohad-Maliki models of Islamic thought and jurisprudence. The *Commentary of the Mishnah* and the *Mishneh Torah* thus infused philosophy with Torah and viewed Torah philosophically, as a system of laws designed to organize society toward perfection and orient the individual toward an enlightened life.

Chapter 3
Loving God with the mind

As a sixteen-year-old rabbinic wunderkind and philosophical prodigy, Moses Maimonides defined humanity's place in the universe in his *Treatise on Logic*: "Rationality we call man's difference, because it divides and differentiates the human species from others; and this rationality, i.e., the faculty by which ideas are formed, constitutes the essence of man." The mature Maimonides followed the medieval Aristotelian doctrine that objects in the physical world ensue from the combination of matter and form. Accordingly, *The Guide of the Perplexed* describes the ultimate potential of fully cultivated rationality, this uniquely human faculty, as streaming from divine emanation to the soul: "this intellect is not a faculty in the body but is truly separate from the organic body and overflows toward it."

The ideal life for Maimonides was the life of the mind, with its relentless pursuit of divine wisdom and illumination. Through them one attains true felicity. To that end he pronounced the credo "heed the truth, whoever may have said it" in the introduction to his eight-chapter essay-preface to his *Commentary on the Mishnah Avot*. What is said matters more than whoever said it. Maimonides construed the rabbinic sages' homiletical lessons of *Mishnah Avot* a component of "practical philosophy" that "leads to great perfection and true happiness"—that is, he read this book of the *Mishnah* as devoted to ethical teachings and rational virtues. He also spelled out his epistemological outlook in the *Letter on Astrology* to the rabbis of Provence in response to their query about the halakhic status of the belief in astrology: "Know, my masters, that it is not proper for a man to accept as trustworthy anything other than one of these three things. The first is a thing for which there is clear proof deriving from man's reasoning—such as arithmetic, geometry, and astronomy. The second is a thing that man perceives through one of the five senses—such as when he knows with certainty that this is red and this is black and the like through the sight of his eye.... The third is a thing that man receives from the prophets or from the righteous." Scientific learning, philosophical inquiry, and religious tradition were the interdependent touchstones of Maimonides' intellectual and spiritual life and his teachings.

Maimonides, the rabbinic scholar, scientist, and philosopher, sought enlightenment and universal truths using methods of inquiry dictated by his time and place. He espoused a conviction shared by select intellectuals in the medieval Islamdom, such as al-Farabi and his Andalusi disciple Ibn Rushd, in theorizing philosophy's symbiotic relationship with revelation and religious tradition. With sufficient aptitude and through a rigorous intellectual regimen one could encounter divine wisdom and strive for human perfection through informed scientific study and contemplation of the cosmos in all its wondrous details. Maimonides had already articulated this agenda in his earliest major work, the *Commentary on the Mishnah*, his initial effort to integrate philosophy with Jewish religious law. Through dedicated moral improvement and concerted intellectual effort, one could approach "the apprehension of God, mighty and magnificent, I mean knowledge of God insofar as this lies within man's power."

Maimonides knew all too well that a large majority of Jews in his world were not equipped to surmount the dialectical pathways of the Babylonian Talmud and rabbinic tradition to discern the Torah's practical standards. Moreover, they were incapable of mastering the intellectual rigors of philosophical training to attain "knowledge of God." For that matter, the limits of rational thought and human knowledge even for the intellectual elite is a persistent theme in the Maimonidean corpus. Yet, he was confident that correct opinions were essential for proper adherence to and understanding of the Law. The Introduction to the First Part of *The Guide of the Perplexed* stipulates that "God, may His mention be exalted, wished us to be perfected and the state of our societies improved by His laws regarding actions. Now this can come about only after the adoption of intellectual beliefs, the first of which being His apprehension, may He be exalted, according to our capacity. This, in its turn cannot come about except through divine science, and this divine science cannot become actual except after study of natural science." So how did Maimonides, the rabbinic authority, propose to enlighten his religious community writ large?

The Hebrew Bible and rabbinic literature are naturally brimming with theological tidings. Yet they scarcely advance statements of creed let alone systematize or codify them, something Maimonides conceded even as he grounded all his teachings in these sacred sources. The presumption of God's existence and Oneness, the repudiation of idolatry, and the authenticity of God's revelation of the Torah to Moses and the people of Israel represent critical exceptions—although Maimonides does not elucidate straightaway what precisely God's existence and Oneness signify. Where would Maimonides place his innovative and audacious presentation of what Jews must know about God? He identified the tenth chapter of the Mishnaic Tractate Sanhedrin, a text of paramount interest to the educated and unlearned alike. Here the Mishnah takes up the nebulous biblical notion of "the end of days" originating with the prophets of ancient Israel. This trope subsequently found a place within the complex schemes of rabbinic eschatology including the concept of "the world to come." The sages sketched the characteristics of the latter otherworldly existence (whose entrance must be earned by righteous life on earth) as follows:

"there is no eating, drinking, washing, anointing, or sexual intercourse; but the righteous sit with crowns on their heads enjoying the radiance of the divine presence."

Maimonides' *Commentary on the Mishnah* Sanhedrin 10, the chapter regarding "those who have a portion in the World to Come" (known by tradition as *Pereq Heleq*), provides a critical examination of the exact nature of the "world to come." It was a contested subject among post-rabbinic Jewish authorities and frequently conflated in the popular imagination with two other rabbinic eschatological ("End Times") concepts, "the Messianic era" and "resurrection of the dead." Relying on the Talmudic passage for support from rabbinic tradition, Maimonides outlines the meta-physical quality of "the world to come" and dissociates that immortal "world" from both "the Messianic era" and "resurrection of the dead."

His bold preface to this chapter of the *Commentary on the Mishnah* culminates in the set of principles never so fully conceived or legally stipulated before in Jewish tradition: "I must now speak of the great fundamental principles of our faith. Know that the masters of Torah hold differing opinions concerning the good which will come to a person as a result of fulfilling the commandments which God commanded us through Moses our Teacher. As a consequence of their different understanding of the problem, they also hold widely different opinions concerning the evil which the transgressor suffers. So much confusion has invaded their opinions that it is almost impossible to find anyone whose opinion is uncontaminated by error.... The world to come is the ultimate end toward which all our effort ought to be devoted.... Nevertheless, even though this is the end we seek, he who wishes to serve God out of love should not serve Him to attain the world to come.... One ought not to busy oneself with God's Torah in order to earn one's living by it; nor should the end of studying wisdom be anything but knowing it. The truth has no other purpose than knowing that it is the truth. Since the Torah is truth, the purpose of knowing it is to do it." For this reason, Maimonides dictates that pursuit of benefit, material or otherwise, from studying and observing the Torah and worshipping God constitutes anthropocentric error bordering on idolatry. He construes the quest for knowledge, apprehending scientific truth, and loving God with the mind as rewards in and of themselves that herald the complete felicity awaiting the worthy in the "world to come." Indeed, loving God with the mind and striving to attain knowledge of God intersect in Maimonides' thought in the nexus of Torah, science, and philosophy.

Maimonides' *Thirteen Principles*, supported with references to the Hebrew Bible, guide the Jew to correct opinions even without elementary training in philosophy. These principles may be divided into three thematic groups: the first five principles concern God; six through nine involve prophecy; and principles ten through thirteen relate to reward and punishment: 1. the existence of God; 2. the absolute and unique unity of God; 3. the incorporeality of God; 4. the eternity of God; 5. God alone is to be worshipped; 6. God communicates to prophets; 7. Moses is the greatest prophet; 8. the Torah was given by God; 9. the Torah is immutable; 10. there is divine providence; 11. there is divine punishment and reward; 12. there will be a Messiah; 13. the dead will be resurrected.

Maimonides' introduction to *Pereq Heleq* became legendary, was translated from Judeo-Arabic into Hebrew, and studied independently as a discrete statement of the fundamental principles of Jewish doctrine. For example, the thirteenth-century Hebrew belletrist Immanuel of Rome composed a 72-line poem based on the thirteen principles and the fifteenth-century Yemeni scholar Hoter ben Solomon wrote a Judeo-Arabic commentary on the Arabic original. *Pereq Ḥeleq*'s credal statement was also popularized in the form of *Maimonides' Thirteen Articles of Faith* and became the lyrical subject of *"Yigdal"* ("The living God be exalted"), a hymn probably authored in fourteenth-century Italy, among nearly 100 religious poems whose subject was Maimonides' "Creed." Subsequently, versions of the poem were incorporated into the synagogue liturgy and chanted by diverse Sephardi, Middle Eastern, and Ashkenazi Jewish communities. Maimonides also included the first four of these principles in the form of the first four of the 613 divine commandments in the *Book of Commandments*, a work appended to the *Commentary on the Mishnah* that also serves as a preparatory bridge or introduction to the *Mishneh Torah*. Most significantly, he presented what he called "fundamental principles" (incorporating the first four of the credos regarding God) prominently in Hebrew for a general audience of Jews everywhere at the very outset of the first book (*The Book of Knowledge*) of his *Code of Jewish Law*, the *Mishneh Torah*.

The impetus for Maimonides' unprecedented efforts in the history of Jewish tradition—mandating Jewish doctrine and delineating all the laws of the Torah in clear Hebrew to make them available to everyone—was his diagnosis of the Jewish community's endemic intellectual and spiritual malaise, its acute ignorance of the Torah properly understood, the many maladies that ensue from warped, distorted understanding of the Law, and the inaccessibility of the details of Jewish law for the many folks lacking rabbinic expertise. He delivers a summary analysis of the Jews' dire predicament in the introduction to the *Mishneh Torah*: "Excessive troubles and distressful times press upon all now, and *the wisdom of our wise men have perished, and the understanding of our prudent men is hidden* [see Isa. 29:14]. Hence those interpretations of responses and laws, which the Geonim compiled and saw fit to rendering obvious, have in our times become difficult. Only a few in number properly understand their meanings. Needless to say, [the same holds for] the Talmud itself.... For they require a broad understanding, a wise soul, and a long time.... On account of this, I, Moses ben Rabbi Maimon, the Spaniard, *roused myself* [see Neh. 5:13], and relying on the Rock (blessed be He), *meditated in all these books* [see Dan. 9:2]....

Accordingly, I have titled this "compilation *Mishneh Torah* [i.e., repetition of the Torah], because a man who first reads the Written Law and after that reads this, will know from it the entire Oral Law and will have no need to read any other book besides them."

The methods Maimonides employed in composing and compiling *The Code*, the work's systematic configuration, and more than a few of its theological details were instigated by developments in twelfth-century Maghribi-Andalusi Islam as well as the legal and theological works of his eastern and Maghribi Jewish predecessors. It was especially imperative, he thought, to remedy the epidemic of ignorance of the Torah, and unwittingly idolatrous notions, inclinations, superstitions, and practices he diagnosed among the Jews of al-Andalus, North Africa, Egypt, the Levant, and Yemen to say nothing of what he heard about the situation in France from his contacts in that land. The ideas in the "Almohad Creed" (*al-'Aqida*) Maimonides encountered during his youth in al-Andalus and the Maghrib provided a prototype for crafting the roster of compulsory precepts and the specific formulations of the "fundamentals" of Jewish belief. Indeed, Maimonides' doctrinal texts are closely related to Almohad thought.

How significant did Maimonides regard these "great fundamental" tenets outlined in the *Commentary on the Mishnah*? In a sense they function as one of the organizing principles connecting all his works in a battle against idolatry in all its insidious forms: "The precept relating to idolatry is equal in importance to all the other precepts put together...hence the inference that acceptance of idolatry is tantamount to repudiating the whole Torah, the prophets and everything that they were commanded, from Adam to the end of time....And whoever denies idolatry confesses his faith in the whole Torah....And this is the fundamental principle of all the commandments." The "great fundamentals" underscore Maimonides' determination to impart rudimentary philosophy to his religious community as an integral part of its system of law.

Maimonides expanded upon the first four "fundamentals" in the first four chapters ("Laws of the Foundational Principles of the Torah") of the first book (*The Book of Knowledge*) of the *Mishneh Torah* where they hew closely to Aristotelian physics and metaphysics while grounded in biblical quotations. Maimonides also hints at their foundational nature in the culminating passage of the *Guide of the Perplexed*, the analytically demanding book formally addressed to his student Joseph ben Judah (originally sent to him seriatim in Aleppo), the select audience of Jewish religious intellectuals of his ilk, and other students of the Torah confounded by their encounter with philosophy: the only virtue worth striving for is "the acquisition of the rational virtues—I refer to the conception of the intelligibles, which teach true opinions concerning the divine things. This is in true reality the ultimate end; this is what gives the individual true perfection, a perfection belonging to him alone; and it gives him permanent perdurance; through it man is man."

By stipulating the Torah's "great fundamental principles" in the *Commentary on the Mishnah* and incorporating four into the *Mishneh Torah* and positioning them at the very beginning of this compendium of Jewish law, Maimonides was, in effect, enacting philosophical tenets in the form of decrees of religious law, just as the Almohads had done. In this respect, like his Andalusi contemporary Ibn Rushd, who also was a jurist and physician as well as a philosopher, Maimonides was a devotee of al-Farabi in reworking his theory of the interdependent relationship between revealed religion and philosophy. Following Bahya ibn Paquda and like Ibn Rushd, Maimonides considered scientific inquiry and contemplation (*i'tibar*) as essential religious obligations inscribed in the Torah. Maimonides found halakhic authority for mandating this practice by explaining how the biblical directive to love God (Deut. 6:5) is achieved by contemplating "His commandments, His injunctions, and His works." To put it another way, loving God is mediated conjointly by religious tradition, science, and philosophy. This legal principle was of such importance to

Maimonides that it is reiterated three times in the *Mishneh Torah* and again in the *Guide of the Perplexed*. Near the beginning of the first book in the *Mishneh Torah* Maimonides explains: "This honored and feared deity—it is a commandment to love Him and to fear Him, as it is said: And thou shalt love the Lord thy God [Deut. 6:5]; and it is said: Thou shalt fear the Lord thy God [Deut. 6:13]. And what is the way to loving Him and fearing Him? When a man reflects upon His wondrous great works and creatures and perceives from them His inestimable and infinite wisdom, he at once loves, praises, glorifies and yearns greatly to know the Great Name...." A subsequent passage of the *Book of Knowledge* reads: "One only loves God with the knowledge with which one knows Him....A person ought therefore to devote himself to the understanding and comprehension of those sciences and studies which will inform him concerning his Master, as far as it lies in human faculties to understand and comprehend—as indeed we have explained in the Laws of the Basic Principles of the Torah."

The conclusion of the fourth chapter of *The Book of Knowledge* revisits the theme of the intimate connection between love of God and knowledge of God: "When a man reflects on these things and acknowledges all created things from angel to sphere [to] man and the like, and sees the wisdom of the Holy One (blessed be He) in all the formed and created things, he increases the love for God. His soul thirsts, his flesh longs to love God (blessed be He)....And furthermore they [these five commandments] are the great good the Holy One (blessed be He) causes to overflow for the betterment of this world so as to come into possession of life in the World to Come. And it is possible for all to know them: adult and minor, man and woman, one with broad intellect and one with narrow."

The Guide of the Perplexed cross-references the *Mishneh Torah*'s injunction to love God with the mind as follows: "We have already explained in *Mishneh Torah* that this *love* becomes valid only through the apprehension of the whole being as it is through consideration of His wisdom as it is manifested in it. We have also mentioned there that the Sages, may their memory be blessed, call attention to this notion." Striving to attain knowledge of God through study and contemplation of all creation, that is, through science and philosophy, is not an innovation or adaptation from the ancient Greeks in Maimonides' telling. Maimonides repurposes an important trope Andalusi Jewish literati applied to the exile-induced lost knowledge of Hebrew language, poetry, poetics, and music that were once prominent in ancient Israel. He asserts that the Israelites originally were privy to science and philosophy with the Revelation at Mt. Sinai. Through exile and the many tribulations it wrought, the safely guarded metaphysical knowledge of "the mysteries of the Torah" dissipated and nearly disappeared among the Jews over time. Maimonides thus frames his effort to educate *The Guide*'s audience as a step in the process of recovering and restoring the wisdom and learning of ancient Israel and the rabbinic sages: "Know that the many sciences devoted to establishing the truth regarding these matters that have existed in our religious community have perished because of the length of time that has passed, because of our being dominated by the pagan nations, and because, as we have made clear, it is not permitted to divulge these matters to all people.... This was the cause that necessitated the disappearance of these great roots of knowledge from the people...."

Returning to the *Mishneh Torah* addressed to the entire religious community, *The Book of Knowledge* ("Treatise One: Laws concerning the Foundations of the Law") begins with the following *halakhot* (laws) in the form of principles: "The foundation of the foundations and the pillar of the sciences is to know that there is a first existent, that he who brings into existence everything that exists. All existent things of heaven and earth and whatever is in between them would not exist but for the true reality of his existence.... 1. Hence His true reality is unlike the true reality of any of them.... 2. This existent, He is God of the world Lord of all the earth…without hand or body.…To know this is a positive commandment, as it is said: *I am the Lord your God* [Exod. 20:2; Deut. 5:6]. Whoever allows the thought to arise that there is some other god besides this one, transgresses a negative commandment, as it is said, *You shall have no other god besides Me* [Exod. 20:3; Deut. 5:7]. And he denies the root, this being the great root upon which everything depends. 3. This God is One.…There is nothing in His oneness like the 'ones' existing in the world. It is not like the 'one' of a species comprising many [discrete] ones; nor is it like the 'one' of a body which is divisible into parts and dimensions. Rather, it is a oneness unlike any other oneness in the world. 4.…And if the Creator were a corporeal body, He would have an end and limit, for it impossible to be a body without an end.…And since the power of our God (blessed be His name) has no end and no pause—for the sphere is eternally revolving—His power is not a physical power.…" The *Mishneh Torah* obliges the individual and community to *know* the "First Existent" (or "Necessary Existent" as the philosophers put it) rather than simply believe "the great root on which everything depends."

Maimonides stipulates that the quantitative aspect of God's oneness, arguably the common person's focus, does not capture the significance of the divine commandment in its totality. The *Mishneh Torah* proceeds to instruct the general reader in detail about the *qualitative* dimension of God's Oneness. It is precisely this singular property that renders erroneous, unthinkable, and—for Maimonides—heretical the religious community's rampant anthropomorphic and imaginative beliefs. Maimonides thus frames the Torah's five primary commandments concerning God (to know there is but one God; there is no other God; to proclaim God's unity; to love God; to fear God) as predicated on cognitive and intellectual processes as mandated by the Torah, not as subjects of blind faith. On the contrary, rational inquiry affirms "true beliefs." These fundamental principles presented as commandments are restated in an analogous passage in the

Book of Knowledge setting forth the "Laws of Repentance" as well as in the *Book of Commandments*.

Ever the perfectionist, especially considering the stakes as he construed them, Maimonides was constantly rethinking and amending his halakhic works, beginning with the *Commentary on the Mishnah* following its "publication" in 1168, not long after he arrived in Egypt. His revisions include correcting errors he attributed to the difficulties encountered on his treacherous eastward journey. Maimonides' modification of one of the thirteen principles figures prominently among the alterations and improvements he made to this text. The addition found in the margins of an autograph manuscript expands upon the principle of God's eternality (principle four) to include "creation out of nothing," contra Aristotle: "Know that the great foundation of the Torah of our Teacher Moses is that the world is created. God formed it and created it after its absolute non-existence, and that you see me steering clear of the eternity of the world according to the philosophers is for absolute proof of His existence, may He be exalted, as I explained and elucidated in *The Guide*." This reconsideration or amendment, known from revelation but not from reason strictly speaking, alludes to *The Guide*'s presentation of the "Account of the Beginning": "I have already made it known to you that the foundation of the whole Law is the view that God has brought the world into being out of nothing."

Maimonides' modern readers have questioned whether this critical textual addition represents a clarification or a revision of his original cosmological and ontological positions, especially since he characteristically took such painstaking care as an author, educator, and communal authority in communicating his thinking, teaching, and halakhic judgment. Maimonides' genuine views on creation as well as divine providence, miracles, and resurrection of the dead are still very much matters of scholarly debate. During his lifetime and ever since he has been subject to critiques resembling al-Ghazali's sharp assault on philosophers and philosophy on three principal counts: they denied God's willful agency in creating the universe; they rejected the idea of a personal deity who interacts with humans; and they repudiated the doctrine of resurrection of the body. Conservative religious scholars in Maimonides' time raised doubts about the authenticity of his commitment to rabbinic tradition's emphasis on the supernatural character of each of these matters. To that end Maimonides felt obliged to compose the *Treatise on Resurrection* in an attempt to dispel his critics' accusations that he did not accept this important rabbinic teaching. Indeed, he repeatedly prompts his audience in the *Treatise on Resurrection* to recall that resurrection is included in the thirteen principles set forth in the *Commentary on the Mishnah*; and in the *Mishneh Torah* its denial precludes "having a portion in the word to come." Maimonides further reminds the reader that resurrection like creation *ex nihilo* and miracles is identified in *The Guide of the Perplexed* as a matter not subject to philosophical proof. At the same time, Maimonides draws a clear distinction in *The Guide* between "true beliefs" and "beliefs that are necessary for the sake of political welfare," opening his reader to questions, doubts, or suspicions about his actual views.

Today, the crux of divergent and incompatible interpretations of Maimonides hinges largely on several critical considerations. Does the reader think of *The Guide* as an intrinsically esoteric work which was crafted calculatingly to obscure the author's real positions or that its esoteric elements and contradictions are designed deliberately to shield common folk from misunderstanding truly profound matters. Does the reader think of Maimonides as a philosopher first and Jew second, a Jew first and a philosopher second, or that he endeavored to present Torah and philosophy as complementary systems and regimens that share the identical goal of striving to know God and imitate "God's ways" as much as humanly possible. Does the reader regard Maimonides' primary religious orientation as orthopraxic (correct conduct), orthodox (correct belief), or both. Maimonides contributed to this paradox too by his cryptic remarks in the Introduction to Part One of *The Guide*: "Thus we have mentioned there [in his legal compositions, the *Commentary to the Mishnah* and the *Mishneh Torah*] that the *Account of the Beginning* is identical with natural science, and the *Account of the Chariot* with divine science; and have explained the rabbinic saying: *The Account of the Chariot ought not to be taught even to one man, except if he be wise and able to understand by himself, in which case only the chapter headings may be transmitted to him* [BT Hagiga 11b; 13a]. And even those are not set down in order or arranged in coherent fashion in this Treatise, but rather are scattered and entangled with other subjects that are to be clarified. For my purpose is that the truths be glimpsed and then again concealed... and which has concealed from the vulgar among the people those truths especially requisite for His apprehension."

The Guide's Introduction delineates seven causes of contradictions in general, three of which concern us here: (2) changes of opinion; (5) pedagogical purposes; and (7) safeguarding esoteric tenets deemed "very obscure matters" (GP 1 Introduction [1:17–20]), later identified as divine attributes, creation, divine governance of the universe and providence, divine knowledge, divine will, and prophecy. Exceptionally perceptive readers can also attribute perceived cleavages between and within Maimonides' rabbinic and philosophical works to his perfectly calibrated differences in perspective, style, emphasis, nuance, and audience as well as to the evolution of his thought.

The *Mishneh Torah*'s first four chapters in the *Book of Knowledge* joining science and philosophy to *halakha* in fact correspond thematically to the opening passages of *The Guide of the Perplexed*. *The Guide*'s stated purpose is to explain "the meanings of certain terms" and "very obscure parables occurring in the books of the prophets but not explicitly identified as such... even when one who truly possesses knowledge considers these parables and interprets them according to their external meaning, he too is overtaken by great perplexity. But if we explain these parables to him or if we draw his attention to their being parables, he will take the right road and be delivered from perplexity." Maimonides however conditions this purpose: "For my purpose is that the truths be glimpsed and then again concealed, so as not to oppose that divine purpose which one cannot possibly oppose and which has concealed from the vulgar among the people those truths especially requisite for His apprehension."

The Guide's first part concerns God, specifically God's existence, unity, incorporeality, eternity, and creation *ex nihilo*; Part 2 presents proofs for God's existence, unity, incorporeality, as well as cosmology, and concludes with prophecy and Moses' uniqueness; Part 3 deals with the prophet Ezekiel's abstruse vision of the "Account/Work of the Chariot," the problem of evil, reward, punishment, the thorny question of divine providence, and the rational basis for all the laws of the Torah. The book concludes with a discussion of the true nature of "The World to Come" that was presented in simpler terms to the religious community at large in the *Commentary on the Mishnah, Pereq Heleq. The Guide*'s tripartite structure and content, addressed to the "perplexed" religious intellectual elite, parallels the corresponding threefold subject cluster of "principles" and "fundamentals" *Pereq Heleq* presents to the popular audience.

The first equivocal biblical terms *The Guide* engages are "image" (*tselem*) and "likeness" (*d^emut*) from the creation account, where God intones, "Let us make man in our image, after our likeness" (Gen. 1:26). The uneducated and misinformed mistakenly understand these terms in a literal sense and conceive of God in corporeal form and thus in human terms. Maimonides demythologizes the Hebrew Bible and the rabbinic sages' homilies by analyzing the lexical ambiguity of these terms and defining them very differently: "The term image ... is applied to the natural form, I mean to the notion in virtue of which a thing is constituted as a substance and becomes what it is. It is the true reality of the thing....In man that notion is that from which human apprehension derives. It is on account of this intellectual apprehension that it is said of man: '*in the image of God created He him*' (Gen. 1:27)." Similarly, humanity's distinguishing feature is its intellect. Humanity's "likeness" to God, such as it is, is entirely intellectual in nature: "As for the term likeness,...it too signifies likeness in respect of a notion....Now man possess as his proprium something in him that is very strange as it is not found in anything else that exists...namely intellectual apprehension.... It was because of this something, I mean because of the divine intellect conjoined with man, that it is said of the latter that he is in the image of God and in His likeness, not that God, may he be exalted, is a body and possess a shape."

The traditional Jewish notion of thirteen "divine attributes" (for instance, compassionate, gracious, and forgiving) inscribed and proclaimed in the Torah (Exod. 34:6–7), is alluded to elsewhere in the Hebrew Bible, discussed in the Talmud, and recited prominently in the holiday and festival liturgy. These "divine characteristics" posed a closely related philosophical problem for Maimonides: their textual and poetic prominence appeared to compromise the doctrine of divine unity. Some contemporary Muslim thinkers confronted an analogous issue in the Islamic tradition of God's 99 (plus one unknown secret) names (e.g., "The Merciful," "The All Knowing"). How to account for the traditional litany of specific divine "appellations" in view of God's eternal, unchanging, absolute perfection? In the first instance, Maimonides marshalled an extremely expedient, oft-repeated Talmudic dictum in confronting the problem of the Hebrew Bible's predications of divine corporeality. He cites the rabbis' maxim at the outset of the *Mishneh Torah*: "all these expressions and their like that are said in the Torah and in the sayings of the prophets are all of them figurative and metaphoric....As to all of it the sages said 'The Torah speaks in the language of men'" (BT Baba Metsi'a 31b; Berakhot 39b; Yevamot 71a) and again in

The Guide of the Perplexed: "You know their dictum that refers in inclusive fashion to all the kinds of interpretation connected with this subject, namely, their saying: *The Torah speaketh....*The meaning of this is that everything that all men are capable of understanding and representing to themselves at first thought has been ascribed to Him as necessarily belonging to God, may He be exalted. Hence attributes indicating corporeality have been predicated of Him in order to indicate that He, may He be exalted, exists, inasmuch as the multitude cannot at first conceive of any existence save that of a body alone....And it shall be demonstrated further on that He, may He be exalted, is not endowed with magnitude, and that in consequence motion does not pertain to Him...all these terms indicative of various kinds of motions of living beings are predicated of God....For motion is an accident attached to living beings. There is no doubt that when corporeality is abolished, all these predicates are abolished."

Part 1, chapters 47–54, of *The Guide* explain in detail that all such divine "attributes" including qualities of character, emotions, or relationships ascribed to God in the Hebrew Bible are neither accidental nor essential but rather are linguistic contrivances to facilitate limited human understanding. Anthropomorphic (having human characteristics) and anthropopathic (having human feelings) representations of God are never to be understood literally. To do so advances the mistaken sense of a composite, changeable, and inconstant deity and violates the reality of the immaterial, absolute, perfect unity of God without any material, spatial, or temporal dimensions. The *Mishneh Torah*, directed to everyone, follows the *Commentary on the Mishnah* in explaining these fundamental principles and asserting that they are central to the Torah's teachings. Religious intellectuals, the principal audience for *The Guide*, should comprehend the truth of these fundamental principles through apprehension and rational demonstration: "For there is no oneness at all except in believing that there is one simple essence in which there is no complexity or multiplication of notions, but one notion only…not divided in any way and by any cause into two notions; and you will not find therein any multiplicity either in the thing as it is outside of the mind or as it is in the mind.…With regard to those three groups of attributes (definitions, accidents, and relations)—which are the attributes indicative of the essence or part of the essence or of a certain quality subsisting in the essence—it has already been made clear that they are impossible with reference to Him, may He be exalted, for all of them are indicative of composition.…" Only actions ascribed to God are valid expressions yet these too are projections, concessions to human language; they represent "attributes of His actions," but are not qualities predicated of God. The sole permissible (and necessary) positive affirmation that can be made of God is God's action in creating the universe.

Finally, the prominence of essential divine attributes in the human imagination, their extensive use in the language of rabbinic tradition, and their limited adoption by Sa'adia Gaon in the Islamic East and Bahya ibn Paquda in al-Andalus led Maimonides, with reservations and restrictions, to follow al-Farabi and Ibn Sina and consider Plotinus' doctrine of "negative attributes" as a counterpart to his notion of "attributes of action": "Know that the description of God…by means of negations is the correct description—a description that is not affected by an indulgence in facile language and does not imply any deficiency with respect to God in general or in any particular mode.…I shall make clear to you that we have no way of describing Him unless it be through negations and not otherwise." For example one might say, "God is not not wise." However, while pointing one in the right direction away from positive attributes, negative attributes also amount to a rhetorical-logical formula and linguistic compromise to accommodate limited human understanding. They fall short of expressing the profound "true reality" in *The Guide*'s intentionally puzzling presentation of what may not and may be said and known about the deity and why. Negative attributes serve as a crutch to "conduct the mind toward the utmost reach that man may attain in apprehension of Him." In the end, because of human shortcomings, Maimonides cites Psalm 65:2 and concludes "silence with regard to You is praise" because "apprehension of Him consists in the inability to attain the ultimate term in apprehending Him."

Part Two of the *Guide of the Perplexed* turns to proofs for the God's existence, unity, incorporeality, creation, and revelation (especially Mosaic revelation), topics addressed in complementary passages of the *Commentary on the Mishnah* and the *Mishneh Torah* devoted to the foundational principles of the Torah. Chapters 32–48 of *The Guide* cover the critical matter of prophecy, a recurrent subject in Maimonides' writings that is addressed in four of Maimonides' "Foundational Principles." He previously took up prophecy in the extensive Introduction to the *Commentary on the Mishnah* devoted to the transmission of the Oral Torah, in additional places of the *Commentary on the Mishnah* on the fundamental principles and the Introduction to the *Eight Chapters*, and in the *Mishneh Torah* "Foundations of the Torah." The subject of prophecy is also treated in the *Letter to Yemen*, the *Essay on Resurrection*, mentioned in *The Guide*'s Introduction as the focus of a book Maimonides once began to write, and extensively in the last section of Part 2 of *The Guide*. The phenomenon of prophecy, especially Moses' prophecy, was of paramount significance to Maimonides' political, ethical, and legal thought because it was the medium through which Moses "received" the Torah, "the Law" in Maimonides' preferred parlance.

What exactly is prophecy for Maimonides? *The Guide*'s opaque discussion is prefigured in the *Commentary on the Mishnah* where prophecy is construed as a natural phenomenon restricted to a select few individuals: "The sixth fundamental principle is prophecy. One should know that among men are found certain people so gifted and perfected that they can receive pure intellectual form. Their human intellect clings to the Active

Intellect, whither it is gloriously raised. These men are prophets; this is what prophecy is." The *Guide of the Perplexed* expands the *Commentary*'s purposefully laconic statement. The prophet's "intellectual faculty" and "imaginative faculty" receives "divine overflow" or emanation (an idea going back to al-Farabi) through the "Active Intellect." "Know that the true reality and quiddity of prophecy consist in its being an overflow overflowing from God, may He be cherished and honored, through the intermediation of the Active Intellect, toward the rational faculty in the first place and thereafter toward the imaginative faculty."

The Hebrew Bible identifies numerous figures as prophets. All but one perceived divine communication in the form of dreams, visions, or voices and belonged to lesser categories in the hierarchy of prophets. Moses was peerless and in a class of his own. He received divine revelation without intercessor and experienced his unique prophecy mediated solely by the "intellectual faculty." In the general introduction to the *Commentary on the Mishnah* that precedes "The Order of Agriculture," Maimonides identifies individuals "fully proficient in learning and completely accomplished in action" as "*al-insan al-kamil*," the person who reached (human) perfection. Accordingly, the seventh Fundamental Principle in the *Commentary on the Mishnah* (*Pereq Heleq*) builds upon the sixth turning specifically to Moses, the epitome of human perfection. It casts Moses as the proverbial *al-insan al-kamil*, much in the way Sufi Muslims from the eleventh century onward, among others, envisioned the prophet Muhammad: "The Seventh Foundation is the prophecy of Moses, our teacher, that is, to affirm that he is the father of all the prophets who preceded and succeeded him; they are all beneath him in rank.... He attained apprehension of Him, may He be exalted, greater than anyone who ever existed or will ever exist. He, peace be upon him, reached the degree of utmost splendor beyond the human.... The first difference of the prophecy [of Moses from the prophecy of other prophets] is that God does not speak with any other prophet except by means of an intermediary, but spoke with Moses directly, as is written 'I speak with him mouth to mouth' [Num. 12:8]."

For *The Guide* Moses' prophecy differed in kind on account of his intellectual perfection: "His [Moses'] apprehension was not like that of the Patriarchs, but greater—nor, all the more, like that of others who came before.... Thus it has been made clear that his apprehension is different from all those who came after him in Israel. . .." Furthermore: "After we have spoken of the quiddity of prophecy, have made known its true reality, and have made it clear that the prophecy of *Moses our Master* is different from that of the others, we shall say that the call to the Law followed necessarily from that apprehension alone. For nothing similar to the call addressed to us by Moses our Master has been made before him by any of those we know who lived in the time between Adam and him; nor was a call similar to that one made by one of our prophets after him. Correspondingly it is a fundamental principle of our Law that there will never be another Law." *The Guide*'s interpretation of the theophany in Exodus 33–34 thus asserts that only Moses attained a higher level of consciousness and was afforded knowledge of "God's ways," that is, God's actions. Moses' singular status among the prophets is essential because it affirms the truth, immutability, and perfection of what he apprehended directly from God—the Law.

The centrality of the intellect and knowledge to human existence and to religious experience and practice also informs Maimonides' perspective of the rationality of the Torah's commandments. Because Maimonides viewed philosophy and the Torah intertwined as repositories of truth, it followed that the Torah's legislation—dietary, family, ethical, criminal, civic, and ritual—was rational in nature. Its regulations, prohibitions, prescriptions, and procedures provide a divine blueprint for administration of an ideal society, for individual wellbeing, and they offer a path toward human felicity. For that matter, Maimonides' *Book of Commandments* likewise took up the conceptual and methodological problems of detailing the divine commandments. With exceptional clarity the *Book of Commandments* delineates their legal categories and demonstrates the rational basis for all the laws of the Torah. The Law relies completely upon philosophical principles and correct opinions in Maimonides' scheme because both lead to knowledge of God and human perfection—the aim of philosophy and divine law in tandem going back to al-Farabi's *Attainment of Happiness*.

The third part of the *Guide*, chapters 25–50, further expounds upon the rationale for the Torah's divine commandments. *The Guide* follows the Written Torah in referring to two classes of laws as *huqqim* ("statutes") or *mishpatim* ("ordinances"). Traditionally, the latter were distinguished as promulgated by God for their obvious rational basis such as the prohibitions against murder and theft. Commandments in the former category were considered divinely decreed but without a discernable rationale such as the laws of ritual purity and impurity. For Maimonides, however, it is inconceivable that God ordains law without design, function, and objective: all the laws God mandates necessarily serve a rational purpose even if it is not always completely apparent. *The Guide* further identifies three categories of laws: opinions, moral qualities, and political civic actions: "Every commandment from these six hundred and thirteen commandments exists either with a view to communicating a correct opinion, or putting an end to an unhealthy opinion, or to communicating a rule of justice, or to warding off an injustice, or to endowing men with a noble moral quality, or warning them against an evil moral quality."

Maimonides views the ancient Israelite cultic system of animal sacrifice the Torah describes in detail through a

6. The *Book of Commandments*, Maimonides' Arabic work enumerating the 613 divine commandments set forth in the Written Torah. This manuscript was copied by a late fifteenth-century Yemeni scribe. His elaborate decoration marks the dividing line in the book between the "positive commandments" and the "negative commandments."

historical-anthropological lens. It was a necessary divine accommodation to the primitive human condition at a particular historical moment in which the people's religious mentality more closely resembled their neighbors'. An early stage in the ancient Israelites' religious development thus required material procedures for their divine service. Only then they became more acquainted with the Law's prescribed path for contemplating and worshipping the One and in the process become "a kingdom of priests and a holy nation" (Exod. 19:6): "For a sudden transition from one opposite to another is impossible. And therefore man, according to his nature, is not capable of abandoning suddenly all to which he was accustomed... and as at that time the way of life generally accepted and customary in the whole world and the universal service upon which we were brought up consisted in offering various species of living beings in the temples.... His wisdom and gracious ruse... did not require that He give us a Law prescribing the rejection, abandonment, and abolition of all these kinds of worship...."

This extended passage divulges the otherwise obscure reasons for divine commandments relating to ancient Israel's cultic edifices (the Tabernacle used by the Israelites during their sojourn in the wilderness; subsequently the Temple constructed by King Solomon in Jerusalem) and their associated sacrificial practices. It includes Maimonides' startling assertions of God's "wily and gracious" "ruse" (Ar. *lutf*; "cunning"), His "first (primary) intention" and "a second intention" for mandating Israelite sacrificial commandments resembling pagan rites: "I know that on thinking about this at first your soul will necessarily have a feeling of repugnance toward this notion and will feel aggrieved because of it...." The cunning benevolence (a tactic that Maimonides himself arguably deployed in his writings) of divine guidance was a historically contingent stratagem for profound religious reform—to gently wean the Israelites of idolatry and cleanse them of its noxious symptoms and effects.

Long before he completed and published *The Guide*, Maimonides twice addressed the subject of how the commandments of the Law promote ethical behavior and human wellbeing. According to The *Book of Knowledge* and the "Eight Chapters" (the introduction to the *Commentary on Mishnah Avot*), the Law anticipates Aristotle's thinking by dictating adherence to the mean and equating the middle temperament and praxis with walking in God's ways: "In the traditions of our prophets and those who transmit our Law, we see these men aiming at the mean and at preserving their souls and bodies in accordance with what the Law requires...if you consider most of the commandments in this way, you will find that all of them discipline the powers of the soul." For Maimonides, the Law delivers prophylactic and therapeutic benefits to the individual and the religious community. In this respect too it is a vehicle for realizing human perfection: "The Law as a whole aims at two things: the welfare of the soul and the welfare of the body. As for the welfare of the soul, it consists of the multitude's acquiring correct opinions corresponding to their respective capacity....As for the welfare of the body, it comes about by the improvement of the ways of living one with another. In this way the preservation of the population of the country and their permanent existence in the same order became possible, so that every one of them achieves the first perfection; I mean also the soundness of the beliefs and the giving of correct opinions through which the ultimate perfection is achieved....The true Law then...is unique—namely, the Law of *Moses our Master*—has come to bring us both perfections, I mean the welfare of the states of people in their relations with one another...and through the acquisition of a noble and excellent character."

The Guide's concluding chapters 50–54 are devoted to what constitutes human perfection, the ultimate form of divine worship, and how to achieve the former and practice the latter. The chapters include Maimonides' famous "Parable of the Palace." The parable enumerates the various types of people in terms of their proximity to the palace's inner courtyard and the king. They range widely in vicinity and immediacy from those outside the capital city, those inside it who turn their backs to the palace, those who seek to reach and enter the palace but never actually see it, those who reach the palace but only walk around it, those who enter the antechamber, those who enter the inner court, to those who enter in the inner court, make another concerted effort and find themselves in the presence of the ruler from afar or nearby.

While the parable is effectively transparent, Maimonides provides the reader with a detailed interpretation, identifying those who inhabit each of the concentric circles from the greatest distance to the ruler's immediate presence. Those outside the capital city, the uncivilized, are at the farthest remove and have no opinions. Those inside the city who turn their backs to the palace have adopted incorrect and dangerous opinions and apparently represent gentiles. Those who seek to reach the palace but never actually gaze upon it are the "multitude of adherents of the Law." Those who reach the palace but only walk around it signify rabbinic jurists with correct beliefs "who do not engage in speculation concerning the fundamental principles of religion." Those who enter the antechambers have "plunged into speculation concerning the fundamental principles of religion" are of different ranks, including, apparently rabbinic scholars who have studied natural science. Those who enter the "inner part of the habitation" "have understood divine science and entered the inner court" are of different grades of perfection, including philosophically minded rabbinic Jews: "He, however, who has achieved demonstration to the extent that that is possible, of everything that may be demonstrated; and who has ascertained in divine matters... everything that may be ascertained... has come to be with the ruler in the inner part of the habitation." The text's elevation of "men of science" over some rabbinic scholars in degree of perfection naturally rankled traditionalists already suspicious of Maimonides' thinking.

At this juncture in decoding the parable Maimonides abruptly turns with a term of endearment directly to his student Joseph and those like him trained in advanced Talmudic studies, the natural sciences, and metaphysics. The master teacher now identifies in greater detail those who merit the very highest classification: "Know, my son.... If, however, you have understood the natural things, you have entered the habitation and are walking in the antechambers. If, however, you have achieved perfection in the natural things and have understood divine science, you have entered in the ruler's palace into the inner court and are with him in one habitation. This is the rank of men of science; they however, are of different grades of perfection. There are those who set their thought to work after having attained perfection in the divine science, turn wholly to God...renounce what is other than He, and direct all the acts of their intellect toward an examination of the beings with a view to drawing from them proof with regard to Him, so as to know His governance of them in whatever way possible. These people are those who are present in the rulers' council. This is the rank of the prophets."

The prophet Moses naturally ranks above them all with respect to propinquity to the divine: "Among them there is he who because of the greatness of his apprehension and his renouncing everything that is other than God...putting questions and receiving answers, speaking and being spoken to in that holy place...." *The Guide* then directs its reader to pursue total devotion to God with "worship of the heart" "proportionate to apprehension" that is, loving God with the mind in what José Faur called "training for intellectual worship."

The Guide's penultimate paragraph refines the intellectualist sense of human perfection predicated on cerebral apprehension of God. Here Maimonides shifts the emphasis on "how to come closer to Him" from a purely intellectual conception to the regimen of training required in complete observance of the Law. He further summons the thinker to social engagement: "It is clear that the perfection of man that may truly be gloried in is the one acquired by him who has achieved, in a measure corresponding to his capacity, apprehension of Him, may He be exalted.... The way of life of such an individual after he has achieved this apprehension, will always have in view loving-kindness, righteousness, and judgment, through assimilation to His actions, may he be exalted, just as we have explained several times in this Treatise."

What is the reader to make of the destabilizing emphasis different passages of *The Guide* seem to place on intellectual, moral, and political definitions of *imitatio dei*? The answer is to be found in an additional factor in Maimonides' understanding of achieving human perfection as articulated in *The Guide*: observance of the Law. Following the Law does not displace the other avenues on the path to human perfection. On the contrary, the Law itself is imbued with theoretical philosophy, moral guidance, and political directive. They are inseparably entwined as means to the same end in Maimonides' view of the ultimate purpose of human life.

Chapter 4
The humanistic rabbi, philosopher, physician

Moses Maimonides was devoted to the serene life of the mind through whose portal he strove for the sublime. Such an individual naturally would seek solitude for study, reflection, and contemplation. Toward the end of *The Guide*, Maimonides advised his reader to follow just such a path: "Thus it is clear that after apprehension, total devotion to Him and employment of intellectual thought in constantly loving Him should be aimed at. Mostly this is achieved in solitude and isolation. Hence every excellent man stays frequently in isolation and does not meet anyone unless it is necessary." Life's realities have a way of compromising an ideal regimen of withdrawal. Rabbinic tradition strongly discouraged private retreat from the community in any case.

Contrary to his counsel to seclude oneself, Maimonides never wavered in his halakhic commitment to live according to a radically different ideal also expressed in the third part of *The Guide*: "It is clear that the perfection of man that may truly be gloried in is the one acquired by him who has achieved, in a measure according to his capacity, apprehension of Him...and who knows his providence extending over His creatures as manifested in the act of bringing them into being and in their governance as it is. The way of life of such an individual...will always have in view *loving-kindness*, *righteousness*, and *judgment*, through assimilation to His actions...." The disparity between the two ideals Maimonides expressed in *The Guide* and his lived life's resemblance to the second rather than the first mirrors the discrepancy between other Muslim, Christian, and Jewish thinkers' philosophical directives and their public experiences.

Compare *The Guide*'s first perspective on human perfection with the practical-philosophical and political agenda of attaining moral virtue articulated in the *Treatise of the Art of Logic*. In that early work (whose authenticity is questioned by several leading readers but embraced by many other experts) Maimonides outlined the individual's self-governance through acquisition of moral virtues, the governance of the household, the governance of the city through imparting to its citizens knowledge of true happiness and how to achieve it, and the governance of the nation by which he meant the exercise of authority in strict accordance with divine commands. Did Maimonides favor a life of contemplation and rational examination of reality, a practical life in pursuit of social and political activity, or neither? The implications of these opposing readings for Maimonides' "true" beliefs are extremely revealing. One school of Maimonidean scholars identify Maimonides as a political philosopher and genuine skeptic who rejected the contemplative life and embraced the active life. Their interlocutors construe the contradictory positions in Maimonides' works as more apparent than real. He was a thinker *and* a social being who balanced the theoretical and practical approaches to a virtuous life in the manner of a prophet.

The demands on Maimonides' time were considerable on account of his towering intellect, achievements, and reputation as a Jewish scholar. Occasionally, the pressure for his attention seemed all-consuming. Consider just his responsibilities as the leading public figure and rabbinic authority of the Jewish community of Cairo and his medical services in caring for patients from all walks of life. The conflict between Maimonides' unrelenting communal and professional duties as an ethical imperative in accordance with the Torah and his dedication to the inner life as a critical religious obligation—what Isadore Twersky deemed the "profound paradox" of his life—was aggravated as his status as an unrivaled rabbinic authority grew beyond measure and especially once his younger brother, David, perished. Maimonides experienced the unexpected, tragic loss of David as a trauma that devasted his psychological and physical wellbeing. He described his debilitating sorrow and what sustained him through it in replying later in life (1185) to a personal letter he received: "And were it not for the Torah, which is my delight, and for scientific matters, which let me forget my sorrow, I would have perished in my affliction [Ps. 119:92]."

Maimonides vividly detailed the daunting burden of his daily late life routine in a letter to his Hebrew translator Samuel ibn Tibbon. The missive successfully deterred Samuel from making the journey from Provence to Egypt to consult with the master over some difficult passages in *The Guide*: "The Creator of the world

7. Ben Ezra Synagogue in Fustat (Old Cairo) was where Judeo-Arabic, Hebrew, and Aramaic texts and documents, including many of Maimonides' writings, were stored in what is known as the Cairo Geniza.

knows how I wrote to you this amount and that I flee from mankind and seek seclusion in a place they are unaware of, sometimes leaning against a wall, sometimes writing while lying because of the great weakness of my body, for its powers have failed and I am old.... But do not hope to study any science or be alone with me for even a single hour, day or night. I dwell in Fustat while the king resides in Cairo.... I have a very difficult assignment with the king. I must see him daily at the at the beginning of the day. When he is weak, or when one of his sons or concubines is ill, I do not leave Cairo, and most of my day I spend in the king's palace. And I must attend to the king's officers every day. One or two officials is invariably ill, and I must administer their medical treatment.

In sum, every day I go up to Cairo early in the morning, and if there is no mishap or incident, I return to Fustat after midday in any case. As soon as I arrive, in a state of hunger, I find all the vestibules [of my home] filled with gentiles, noble and common, judges and magistrates, a mixed multitude, who know the time of my return. I dismount from my riding animal, wash my hands, and go out to them to persuade them to wait for me while I have a light repast, which I do from time to time. I then go out to heal them and write [prescriptions] for them. They come in and out until night, and at times, by faith in the Torah, until the end of two hours into the night [around 8:00 P.M.]. I speak with them while lying down because of great fatigue.

When night falls I am so utterly exhausted that I cannot speak. The result is that no Israelite can speak with me or meet me except on the Sabbath. Then they all come after the [morning] prayer. And I direct the community concerning what they should do all week. They study light things until noon, and then go one their way. Some of them return and study again until the evening prayer. This is my daily schedule, and I have only told some of what you would see, with the help of God (may He be exalted)." We read similar complaints about Moses' taxing schedule, physical exhaustion, and absence of opportunities for leisure in his correspondence with R. Jonathan ha-Cohen and the rabbis of Lunel and in the *Letter on Astrology*.

Maimonides interacted regularly with Muslim, Christian, and Jewish doctors in Cairo's sophisticated hospital and clinical medical services system including Hibbat Allah ibn Jumay', also known as al-Shay<u>kh</u> al-Muwaffaq, an illustrious Jewish colleague who served as the sultan Saladin's personal physician. In that network Maimonides joined an elite class of prominent physicians. They were viewed widely as repositories of scientific and philosophical knowledge whose learning transcended confessional boundaries. At the same time Moses and subsequently his son, Abraham, like Ibn Rushd, belonged to an even more select group of physician-scientist-philosophers who were the foremost scholars of their

8. This Judeo-Arabic fragment discovered in the Cairo Geniza is from Maimonides' *Regimen on Health*. He wrote the work in 1198 for an Egyptian sultan who suffered from depression and resultant physical symptoms.

religious communities' sacred law. Maimonides urged his closest disciple, Joseph ben Judah ibn Simon, in Aleppo to earn a living by teaching medicine while "occupying yourself in the true study of the Torah." It is uncertain whether Maimonides taught medicine himself.

His extant corpus of four major medical works (*Medical Aphorisms, Commentary on Hippocrates' Aphorisms, On Poisons, Compendia from the Works of Galen*) and six minor ones (*On Coitus, On the Regimen of Health, On the Causes of Symptoms, Glossary of Drug Names, On Hemorrhoids, On Asthma*) testifies to Moses' wide-ranging theoretical as well as practical interest in medicine and pharmacology. These studies reflect Maimonides' extensive knowledge of Hippocrates (in Arabic translation), the Iraqi al-Razi (Rhazes), one of the foundational figures of Islamic medicine; Ibn Zuhr (Avenzoar) among the Andalusi scholars he especially favored, the Bukharan Ibn Sina, and above all Galen (in Arabic translation). Indeed, Maimonides and Ibn Sina, author of *The Book of Healing*, followed Galen's statement that an excellent physician must be a philosopher too.

For Maimonides the noble practice of medicine conferred internal and external benefits and was imbued with profound religious significance, as his admirer al-Harizi expressed in verse after his death:

> God sent Moses the prophet to dispel the shadows and spread
>   guidance,...
> After Moses had been gathered unto his Lord,
> He who had been a light in which guidance was found.
> [Maimonides] arose to revive His law, a leader who from birth has
>   been followed.
> He was named Musa (the "healer" in Aramaic) for through him the
>   Torah heals,
> For he became a panacea for all ills.
> He resuscitated the sciences and wounds mended,

The sick who ceased to ail, he tended.

He wrote compositions which embrace knowledge.

Yea, wherefore is he who can know of what he innovated.

For he was unique, the noblest in existence.

How difficult for us that he is extinguished,

For after him virtue vanished,

And the sword of dignity reverted to the sheaf.

May God be pleased with him,

And accept from him the noble edifice which he built for us.

Maimonides' *Eight Chapters* opens a window into his perspective on the study of medicine as a template for ethical conduct: "the study of medicine has a very great influence upon the acquisition of the virtues and of the knowledge of God, as well as upon the attainment of true spiritual happiness. Therefore, its study and acquisition are pre-eminently important religious activities, for by it one learns to weigh one's deeds, and thereby human activities are rendered true virtues."

The *Eight Chapters* and the *Mishneh Torah* are suffused with medical idioms and images and draw upon the physician's humanistic perspective on the healing purpose of the Torah's legislation. These texts view the stages of human development as a hierarchical series progressing from bodily wellbeing, ethical goodness, to intellectual perfection and envision the dependence of the latter on the former. For instance, "Laws Concerning Ethical Dispositions," the first chapter of the second section of the *Book of Knowledge*, identifies the injunction to "walk in God's ways" with the Aristotelian principle of avoiding excess and deficiency as the virtuous human state. It also frames "the right path" and "balanced behavior" in curative terms: "The sick in body taste what is bitter as sweet and what is sweet as bitter.... Similarly, people whose souls are sick crave and relish the vices, disrelish the good way, are loath to follow it, and find it onerous on account of their sickness.... And what is the remedy for the sick in soul? Let them go to the wise, who are the physicians of souls; they will heal them of their sickness through the dispositions in which they train them, until they have turned them to the good way."

Chapter 4 of this section of the *Mishneh Torah*'s first book comprises a detailed manual for healthful behaviors rooted in medical knowledge including recommendations for diet, sleep, elimination, hygiene, exercise, and bathing. It concludes with a directive regarding what the wise require to live properly in a city: "No disciple of the wise may live in a city that is unprovided with the following ten officials and institutions, namely: a physician, a surgeon, a bath-house, a lavatory, a source of water supply such as a stream or a spring, a synagogue, a school teacher, a scribe, a treasurer of charity funds for the poor, a court that has the authority to punish with stripes and imprisonment."

The depth of Maimonides' religious humanism is palpable in his treatment of patients without regard for their socioeconomic status or religious affiliation. It is also evident in his relationship with advanced students of Torah and philosophy, notably Joseph ben Judah. Maimonides' mindset regarding the dignity of human beings informs many of his *responsa* on matters of Jewish law. On sensitive family issues, for example, he validated the principle that a merchant "may not travel without her (his wife's) permission" on account of her conjugal rights. Regarding the demands of commerce he accommodated Jewish business partnerships with Muslims. He displays profound compassion in occasional pastoral epistles to individuals, for instance to psychologically distressed proselytes, to groups like the rabbis of Lunel, and to entire communities such as the Jews of Yemen in desperate need of wise and palliative counsel.

The *Mishneh Torah*'s stipulations for judges and community leaders reflect similar concerns for respecting the public through unassuming behavior: "It is forbidden to lead the community in a domineering and arrogant manner. One should exercise one's

9. An autograph responsum (answer to a legal query) by Maimonides, one of many such documents discovered in the Cairo Geniza. The final word of the last line (reading from right to left) is "Moshe," Moses.

authority in a spirit of humility and reverence. The man at the head of the congregation who arouses excessive fear in the hearts of the members thereof for any but a religious purpose will be punished.... He is also forbidden to treat people with disrespect thought they be ignorant." Perhaps the only social sphere in which Maimonides' enlightened religious humanism fell decidedly short of our present-day standards and expectations is when it came to women, consistent with the patriarchal tendencies of the rabbinic tradition he inherited and the philosophical and medical thinking of his time and place.

Maimonides' letters to Obadiah the Proselyte and Joseph ibn Jabir offer excellent illustrations of the master's empathy for people troubled by what they (mis)perceived to be their inferior religious status. Obadiah wrote to Maimonides with three questions in mind. The first letter concerned the nature of Obadiah's status as a Jew: was he permitted to recite the words "*our* God and God of *our* fathers," "who brought *us* out of the land of Egypt," in the congregational prayer and other such prominent phrases in the canonical liturgy? Maimonides replies in the affirmative but does not leave it at that. He envelops his ruling within a psychologically astute response to the puzzled convert's query because he senses the heart of the matter extends well beyond the legal issue. Maimonides counts the righteous proselyte among the descendants of Abraham *and* elevates his station in relation to God: ". . . whoever adopts Judaism and confesses the unity of the Divine name, as it is prescribed in the Torah, is counted among the disciples of Abraham our Father, peace be with him.... In the same way he converted future generations through the testament he left his children and household after him. Thus Abraham our Father... is the father of his pious posterity who keep his ways, and the father of his disciples and of all proselytes who adopt Judaism.... Do not consider your origin as inferior. While we are descendants of Abraham, Isaac, and Jacob, you derive from Him through whose word the world was created. As is said by Isaiah:

'One shall say, I am the Lord, and another shall call himself by the name of Jacob' (Is. 44:5)."

Obadiah's third question involved the monotheistic standing of Muslims according to *halakha*. But the social circumstances underlying the question reported by the presumably Muslim convert led Maimonides back to Obadiah's worthy status as a righteous proselyte. A local rabbi indignantly contradicted Obadiah's correct assertion that Muslims are not idolaters. Maimonides replied: "When your teacher called you a fool for denying that Muslims are idolaters he sinned grievously, and it is fitting that he ask your pardon, though he be your master...was he intoxicated that he forgot the thirty three passages in which the Law admonishes concerning "stranger" [understood as converts]? For even if he had been in the right and you in error it was his duty to be gentle; how much more, when the truth is with you and he was in error!...And how great is the duty which the Law imposes on us with regard to proselytes. We are commanded to honor and fear our parents; we are ordered to hearken to the prophets. A man may honor and fear and obey without loving. But in the case of 'strangers' we are bidden to love with whole force of our heart's affection."

Maimonides' response to Joseph ibn Jabir draws on a similar psychological and rhetorical strategy. Ibn Jabir, a resident of Baghdad who knew Arabic and studied the *Commentary on the Mishnah* zealously, fretted that he was unable to study the *Mishneh Torah* in its original Hebrew. Joseph refers to himself as "'*am ha-aretz*" (an ignoramus; lit. "the people of the land"), a frequently pejorative appellation the rabbinic sages had used to connote the uneducated masses or common folk. Maimonides was certainly an intellectual elitist and expressed utter disdain for the ignorant, unenlightened, and misinformed in *The Guide* and elsewhere. And yet, the reader encounters another side of Maimonides in the letter: the sensitive teacher-educator who always meets those who seek his guidance and support with understanding, compassion, and encouragement: "First of all, I must tell you, may the Lord keep and increase your welfare, that you are not justified in regarding yourself as an *am-ha-aretz*. You are our beloved pupil; so is everybody who is desirous of studying even one verse or *halakhah*. It makes also no difference whether you study in the holy language, or in Arabic or Aramaic; it matters only whether it is done with understanding...for the advancement of learning is the highest commandment. I say, therefore, in general that you must not belittle yourself nor give up the intention of improving....If you want to study my work you will have to learn Hebrew little by little. It is not so difficult as the book is written in an easy style, and if you master one part you will soon be able to understand the whole work."

Maimonides' ambient empathy for a deeply troubled community permeates his pastoral communication with the Jews of Yemen, much as his earlier "Letter on Martyrdom" sought to bolster and buoy the Jews of al-Andalus and the Maghrib beset by Almohad persecution. Before Saladin's brother conquered Yemen in 1173, the Jews of that land found themselves besieged under Zaydi Shi'a rule and its forcible diktat they convert to Islam, contrary to Islamic law. They were further disoriented and divided about the appearance of a false messiah in their midst and some of their scholars' espousal of astrology. Others lost faith altogether and found Islam sufficiently familiar and appealing to provide relief from their suffering. Jacob ben Nathanel Fayyumi, one of the Yemenis' desperate leaders, turned to Maimonides for guidance in confronting this existential communal crisis. Moses responded with the *Epistle to Yemen*, one of his best-known and frequently cited compositions. This classic text deftly balances the rhetoric of critique, counsel, instruction, anodyne consolation, and soothing hope. It demonstrates, among other things, the political philosopher's psychological insight and sensitivity alongside the rabbinic master's profound concern and care for the spiritual and physical wellbeing of a remote branch of his religious community, especially its common folk addressed as "we" (although this manner of expression was typical of Andalusi Arabic).

The Arabic *Epistle*'s introduction is composed in highly stylized ornate biblical Hebrew. It begins in a warmly personal tone: "To the honored, great, and holy master and teacher Jacob, the kind, dear, and revered sage (may his Rock preserve him), son of the honored, great, and holy master and teacher Nathanel Fayyumi...." Maimonides identifies the *Epistle*'s intended audience as encompassing the entire Yemeni Jewish community. Nathanel is the conduit for disseminating the *Epistle*: "I have seen fit to write the response in the language and idiom of Kedar [i.e., Arabic] so that he may run that reads it, all of the people, including the children and the women—for all your communities should understand the response to its topics." Indeed, its message is directed to and relevant for the entire Jewish people scattered in exilic lands: "Now then, O our brethren, all Israel dispersed to the ends of the earth, you must fortify one another. Your elders should guide your young, and your elite should guide your common folk. Let all your community consent to the immutable and irreplaceable verity, and to the propagation of the truth that shall never fail or falter. It is that God, the Exalted, is one unlike other ones. And Moses, His prophet and spokesman, is the master and most perfect of all the prophets...." The body of the *Epistle* concludes with additional instructions to Jacob: "I would request that you send a copy of this letter to each and every community, rural and urban, in order to brace their faith and steady their feet. Read it publicly so that you may become one of *those who bring the many to righteousness* [Dan. 12:3]."

The *Epistle* offers a master class in text-based education and in spiritually empowering the distraught multitude as well as the perplexed and dispirited rabbinic elite responsible for the community's wellbeing. With this dual audience in mind,

Maimonides deploys language that is concurrently clear and suggestive. The *Epistle*'s core reviews the Yemenite Jews' plight in historical perspective with a critical emphasis on Moses as the greatest prophet and the Law of Moses as indispensable. The text's pedagogic method revolves around how to read the Hebrew Bible, which he cites copiously and parses confidently along with doctrinal references to the *Mishneh Torah*. Maimonides reminds the Yemenites that the Hebrew Bible's prophesies foretold the Jews' history of trials and tribulations along with divine assurance of their survival and ultimate deliverance: "So rely upon these true texts, O our brethren, and be not alarmed by the succession of persecutions and the power over us or the weakness of our community. All this is to test and purify...."

Maimonides explains that the Jews' destiny as the sole recipients of divine Law ("What great nation has laws and rules as perfect?" citing Deut. 4:8), marks them as unique and consequently subjects them to envy and hostility. Here, the *Epistle* draws a distinction between Israel's political adversaries and its intellectual rivals through history. Maimonides deems Christianity and Islam, the latest in a sequence of intellectual and spiritual rivals, imitative religions while he reckons Christendom and Islamdom political antagonists. Referring to Islamdom, Maimonides observes, "Never has a nation arisen against Israel more harmful than it, nor one which went so far to debase and humiliate and to instill hatred toward us as they have." This judgment certainly applied to Moses' time in the West under the Almohad Berbers and the Yemenis' predicament under two heterodox Islamic dynasties. Nevertheless, Maimonides' testimony of his experiences in Fatimid and Ayyubid Egypt contradicts the *Epistle's* oft-cited appraisal of Jewish life in Islamdom.

Passages of the *Epistle* are also addressed directly to the Yemenis' rabbinic intellectual leaders. It takes them to task for their misguided recourse to astrology and enabling belief in a scarcely educated messianic pretender. They failed in their primary obligation as scholars to educate and guide their community according to the Torah. The *Epistle* reminds its audience that the rabbinic sages strictly prohibited messianic speculation and that in any case such conjectures are futile: "The precise time is unknowable." And yet, Maimonides transgresses this rabbinic prohibition to rally the people to study and observe the Torah. He discloses that his family possessed an esoteric messianic tradition, and he divulges its inspirational and reassuring message: before long divine prophecy will be renewed, an unmistakable sign of the impending messianic age. When the Messiah soon appears, the Jews will be delivered from foreign domination and their exile will come to an end. Then again, Maimonides cautions the Yemenite community that "God is the best knower of the truth," a prevalent Arabo-Islamic aphorism. All in all, the *Epistle to Yemen* reveals its author's emotional intelligence and capacity to nurture hope in dire circumstances. It is perfectly calibrated to transform and transcend the Jews' suffering by underscoring its prediction in prophecy and by assigning it meaning in the divine scheme of history. Unfortunately, there is every indication that many Yemenite Jews abandoned hope for eventual redemption despite Maimonides' salutary intervention.

Contrary to his stated desire to achieve a life of serenity, Maimonides was drawn into predictable controversies because of his intellectual ambition and pedagogical determination to illuminate his entire religious community. More than a few Talmudic scholars blasted Maimonides on account of the *Mishneh Torah*'s audacious nature. Meir Halevi Abulafia of Toledo (known in Jewish tradition as Ramah) and Abraham ben David of Posquières (known by the acronym Rabad) were among the foremost rabbinic critics of Maimonides' *Code* even as the latter evinced respect for his halakhic acumen. Abraham ben David set the agenda for subsequent *Mishneh Torah* criticism. Specifically, he decried the work's absence of Talmudic and post-Talmudic rabbinic sources and its supposed purpose in serving as the final authority on Jewish law. The two scholars also assailed Maimonides for allegedly denying the rabbinic doctrine of resurrection of the dead and, in the case of Abulafia, rejecting Maimonides' emphasis on intellectual immortality as the ultimate end of human existence.

Maimonides' correspondence with the rabbis of Provence indicates that he was supremely self-confident and welcomed appropriate discussion of and debate over his works. But polemical disputes concerning the nature of the *Mishneh Torah* and the orientation of *The Guide of the Perplexed* engulfed him. For one, the *Mishneh Torah* violated the rabbinic rule against committing the Oral Torah to writing. Rabbis from Provence to Baghdad vehemently complained (with justification, since Maimonides declares as much in *The Code*) that Maimonides intended to replace the Talmud with a uniform code of Jewish law, eliminating the need to study the Talmud and depriving scholars of the opportunity to engage in the centuries-long process of deriving practical law. When his devotee Joseph ben Judah ibn Simon reported that some individuals were averse to the *Mishneh Torah*, Maimonides responded with a fourfold justification, including recognition that he expected its negative reception in some misguided and resentful quarters.

Maimonides' exposition of the philosophical foundations of the Law at the outset of "The Book of Knowledge" also generated opposition to the *Mishneh Torah* as an alarming innovation as did his intellectual interpretation of "the World to Come" set forth in "The Laws of Repentance." Because of the latter, Maimonides' suspected, but unstated, interpretation of the rabbinic doctrine of corporeal resurrection drew intense scrutiny. The head of the Baghdad rabbinic academy, Gaon Samuel ben 'Eli, who held authority over the Jewish communities of the Levant, Egypt, and Yemen, viewed the great Maimonides as a political rival who challenged the Gaon's fundraising excesses, authoritarian leadership, and limited curriculum of study. Samuel seized upon the opportunity to become a public critic of his formidable competitor for communal leadership and composed a treatise explaining physical resurrection as the reward awaiting the righteous in "the World to Come." He aimed to incite opposition to Maimonides by drawing attention to the omission of resurrection in *The Code*'s explication of "the World to Come," to Maimonides' arguably nonliteral view of bodily resurrection, and his characterization of "the World to Come" as a purely intellectual conjunction with the divine. Joseph ben Judah ibn Simon was so incensed by the attack on his sage mentor that he came to Maimonides' defense with an intemperate letter entitled *The Silencing Epistle Concerning the Resurrection of the Dead.* In a personal message, Maimonides advised Joseph, whom he affectionately called "my dear son," to maintain his composure and remain undisturbed by provocation.

Maimonides responded to Samuel ben 'Eli's polemic with an open letter in the form of the "Treatise on Resurrection," which claims to offer little new on the subject. As ever, the educator's voice permeates the text: "Know, o thou man of speculation, that our aim in this treatise is the clarification of what we ourselves believe concerning this foundation.... There is nothing at all in this Treatise in addition to what we said ... but a repetition of matters and a popular [lit. vulgar] elaboration, and an additional explanation that the women and ignorant will understand, nothing more." The *Treatise* reviews Maimonides' opinions on "the End of Days" and the nature of divine reward and punishment, presented previously in the *Commentary on the Mishnah*, the *Mishneh Torah*, and *The Guide of the Perplexed*. Maimonides subtly calibrates his prescriptions for therapy of the soul in these works. He designs his treatments to cure the entire Jewish community (thus the inclusion of "the women and ignorant") of endemic theological error and superstitions, remedy its religious intellectuals' uncertainty, and lead every individual to apprehension of the Creator insofar as possible depending on their capacity to reason, their level of education and sophistication.

According to the *Treatise on Resurrection*, the ostensibly learned "jurists of the law" such as Samuel ben 'Eli, completely misread or misinterpreted his works. Their thinking about the body, soul, and intellect is confused and their reliance on rabbinic homilies in forming and supporting their opinions is completely unfounded. Maimonides frames a sharp retort to his adversaries in terms of the intentionality that is critical to serving God and the religious community rather than seeking "reward or honor from human beings." He also reasserts his opinion that the rabbinic doctrine of resurrection ("The righteous whom the Holy One, blessed be He, will resurrect, will not revert to dust" [BT Sanhedrin 92a]) is fundamental but neither demonstrable nor "the final end" from which it is distinct: "The world to come is the reward above which there is no reward and the good beyond which there is no good. We also explained there that bodies do not exist in the World to Come since they have already said: 'In it there is neither eating nor drinking nor copulation' [BT Berakhot 17a]."

The *Treatise on Resurrection* also addresses a series of inquiries and critiques from figures in Damascus, Yemen, and Baghdad regarding the *Mishneh Torah* and its treatment of the subject. The text proceeds to confront the question of why the Written Torah does not mention resurrection and parses prophetic and other writings in the Hebrew Bible that appear to deny it. The sole exception is an allusion to bodily resurrection in the late biblical book of Daniel (12:2; 12:13). The *Treatise* affirms the rabbinic doctrine of resurrection required by tradition and communal consensus as a rare miraculous suspension of the natural order. The text concludes its relatively uncomplicated and superficial presentation by recapitulating its rationale and acknowledging its primarily popular, uneducated audience. Yet Maimonides' secondary purpose is to limit the obsessive attention bodily resurrection receives and direct the mindfulness of learned people toward ultimate existence in "the World to Come."

With the *Treatise on Resurrection*, the *Code of Jewish Law*, the *Guide of the Perplexed*, the *Letter to Yemen*, his *responsa*, and occasional writings, Moses Maimonides attained a unique stature among the Jews of Islamic and Mediterranean lands as a lawgiver, leader, counselor, doctor, scientist, intellectual, philosopher, physician of the soul, and religious humanist of the first order.

Chapter 5
Turning the parochial into the universal

Maimonides' humanistic inclination is perceptible in his approach to religion and religious difference. The introductory essays to the *Commentary on the Mishnah* and the *Mishneh Torah* document the transmission of the Oral Law going back to Moses and the Revelation at Mt. Sinai down through the Talmudic sages and leaders of the Iraqi and Palestinian rabbinical academies. This age-old chain of conveyance affirmed the reliability of the laws that follow in the *Commentary* and *The Code*, contrary to polemical Karaite Jewish and Islamic assertions that rabbinic tradition was fabricated. In addition to his role as a historian of rabbinic tradition, Maimonides was an anthropologist of religion, using methods of inquiry we think of as historicizing to understand the scourge of idolatry, monotheism's regression to it, and the arduous evolution of monotheism's break from it.

Maimonides' understanding of the biblical phrase "in God's image," which he discussed at the outset of *The Guide of the Perplexed*, informed his religious humanism and universalism as much as his orientation as a physician, scientist, and philosopher. Classical rabbinic formulations such as "beloved and precious are human beings created in the image of God" (Mishnah *Pirqei Avot* 3:18) and "one who saves a single human life is as if one saved a whole human world" (BT Sanhedrin 4:5) supported such a humanistic attitude. To the same end, the *Mishneh Torah* enumerates the seven all-embracing laws the rabbinic sages recounted as decreed for the biblical figure Noah and therefore ordained for all of humankind to observe (BT Sanhedrin 56a): establish a system of laws; do not curse God; do not practice idolatry; do not engage in illicit sexual relations; do not engage in bloodshed; do not rob; do not eat the flesh of a living animal. Maimonides writes in *The Code*: "A heathen who accepts the seven commandments and observes them scrupulously is a 'righteous heathen,' and will have a portion in the world to come, provided he accepts them and performs them because the Holy One, blessed be He, commanded them in the Law and made known through Moses, our teacher, that the observance thereof had been enjoined upon the descendants of Noah even before the Law was given."

Maimonides' reading of the Torah's second creation narrative (Gen. 2) in *The Guide of the Perplexed* and the *Mishneh Torah* considers Adam and Eve as exemplars of the natural, monotheistic state of humanity. During the time of Enosh (Gen. 5), he says, human worship became corrupted and regressed initially from monotheism to star veneration and then to various forms of pagan idolatry. Only a few individuals, such as Noah, Shem, and 'Ever (the ancestor of the Hebrews), recognized or knew the Eternal. Monotheism was rediscovered by the patriarch Abraham, who ascertained truth through intellectual effort, proclaimed God's existence, and educated his family and others. Moses and the Torah represent the culmination of the process of recovery to establish "a community of knowers of God" protected by the Law from idolatry's infectious contagion. However, in Maimonides' view the Israelites found "knowing" an incorporeal Deity such an abstract challenge that they required a divine "concession" for expressing their veneration. It took the form of worship customary to the pagans of their time and place—the Torah's cultic system of animal sacrifices.

Maimonides viewed the course of history as inexorably leading humanity in the messianic age back to its original recognition of the One God. He included the doctrine of the messiah in *Commentary on the Mishnah*'s thirteen foundational principles and catalogued its details in the *Book of Judges*, "Laws Concerning Kings and Wars," the fourteenth and concluding book and chapter of the *Mishneh Torah*. He demystified, naturalized, and detached the concept of the messianic age from prevailing superstitious ideas and "End Times" illusions: "Do not think that in the days of the Messiah any of the laws of nature will be set aside, or any innovation be introduced into creation. The world will follow its normal course.... Said the Rabbis: The sole difference between the Messianic days is delivery from servitude to foreign powers [BT Sanhedrin 91b]." The universalistic, utopian vision further elides any difference between Israel and the "nations": "The Sages and Prophets did not long for the days of the Messiah that Israel might exercise dominion over the world, or rule over the heathens, or be exalted by the nations, or that it might eat and drink and rejoice. Their aspiration was that Israel be free to devote itself to the Law and its wisdom, with no one to oppress or disturb it, and thus be worthy of life in the world to come. In that era there will be neither famine nor war, neither jealousy nor strife. Blessings will be abundant, comforts within the reach of all. The one preoccupation of the whole world will be to know the Lord. Hence Israelites will be very wise, they will know the things that are now concealed and will attain an understanding of their Creator to the utmost capacity of the human mind, as it is written: For the earth shall be full of the knowledge of the Lord, as the waters cover the sea [Isa. 11:19]."

Maimonides' ecumenical understanding of the Torah and its purpose compelled him to reassess the biblical notion of "chosen-ness" that became a critical touchstone of post-biblical Jewish tradition. It is reflected conspicuously in the Talmudic sages' midrashic literature, theology, and allegorical reading of the biblical *Song of Songs* about the love between God and the people of Israel. Israel's chosen-ness was textualized prominently in rabbinic liturgy and subsequently in *piyyutim* (religious poems) added to the synagogue service and in devotional poetry. The peoples of the ancient Near East all conceived of themselves as exclusively chosen by their respective deities. In the case of the Israelites, the idea of their "election" by the "God of Israel" was predicated on God's covenant with Abraham ("For I have singled him out, that he may instruct his children and his posterity to keep the way of the Lord, by doing what is just and right," Gen. 18:19; cf. Neh. 9:7), introduced in Exodus 19:5 ("Now then, if you will obey Me faithfully and keep My covenant, you shall be My treasured possession [*sᵉgullah*] among all the peoples"), reiterated in Deuteronomy 26:18–19 ("And the Lord has affirmed this day that you are, as promised, God's treasured people [*'am sᵉgullah*] who shall observe all the divine commandments. And that [God] will set you in fame and renown and glory high above all the nations that [God] has made…") and referenced poetically in Psalm 135:4 ("For the Lord has chosen Jacob for Himself, Israel, as His treasured possession") among many biblical passages designating Israel's special relationship with God.

One prominent rabbinic interpretation of Israel's "treasured," "beloved," or "singular" status suggested this bond existed before Creation and is therefore eternal. The more common opinion of the sages regarded the attachment between God and the Jewish people as historical in accordance with the plain sense of the Written Torah's narrative. The obligations of this reciprocal relationship were formalized in the Torah's legal stipulations of the covenant. Over centuries of exile and dispersion the Jews' sense of their "election" delivered consolation, inspired psychological uplift, and conferred imagined agency to them in counterpoint to their humiliating minority status in Christendom and Islamdom and their political powerlessness. Their divine chosen-ness provided reassurance in the prophetic promises of restoration when the Messiah (finally) appears, gathers the dispersed of Israel, and reestablishes their sovereignty in the land of Israel.

How did Maimonides interpret the potent idea of Israel's divine "election"? His Andalusi predecessor, Judah Halevi, developed an essentializing scheme drawn from terminology and concepts prominent in Shi'i Islam according to which a succession of individuals from Adam to Jacob were divinely chosen and their religious "uniqueness" transmitted by heredity. In due course the Israelites and the Jews were bestowed supernaturally with an exclusive, vital endowment —the "divine faculty" or "divine order" (Ar. *al-amr al-ilahi*). Halevi's innovative notion of this godly "genetic receptor" represented a radical statement of an embodied-spiritual Jewish particularism beyond what the Hebrew Bible or rabbinic tradition envision. It is the sign of a primordial and essential relationship between God and the Jews that marks them as somewhat distinct from the rest of humanity. Proselytes, while Jews in every other respect, are excluded from receiving this patrimony and therefor incapable of achieving prophecy or attaining religious perfection. For Maimonides, by contrast, there could be nothing inherently worthy or unique about the Jews either as individuals or as a religious community; they enjoy no special ontological status among the nations. Rather, acceptance of the Torah and adherence to the divine commandments, not anything intrinsic to Israel, set the Jewish religious community apart. And even then, Israel's covenantal relationship with God is qualified as conditional. It is entirely contingent on observance of the Torah ("if...then" as in Exodus 19:5) and on choosing to fulfill the religious obligation to study and teach it.

Despite or precisely because of the significant place "election" occupies in Jewish tradition and in Halevi's amplified and unbounded version, Maimonides barely mentions the biblical notion or rabbinic elaboration of chosen-ness. His near silence on this subject is deliberate, suggestive, and speaks volumes in repudiating Halevi's construct. Maimonides repeatedly emphasizes "The Law" the people received rather than the people themselves as the source of Israel's distinction, such as it is: "This is—may God save us and you—the true and valid religion, revealed to us by [Moses] the chief of all the prophets, former and latter, by means of which of which God has distinguished us from all of mankind, as he says: 'Yet it was to your fathers that the Lord was drawn in His love for them, so that he chose you, their lineal descendants, from among all the peoples' [Deut. 10:15]. This was not by your merit, but by favor and grace on account of our ancestors having known Him and obeyed Him, as He, the Exalted, says: 'It was not because you were more numerous than any other people that the Lord set his heart on you and chose you—for you were the fewest of all peoples' [Deut. 7:7]. This is because he has singled us out by His laws and ordinances, and our preeminence over others was evident in His rules and regulations as He, the Exalted, says recounting His loving-kindness to us: And what great nation is there that has statutes and ordinances as perfect [Deut. 4:8]."

Maimonides' portrait of the patriarch Abraham as a natural philosopher who discerned and apprehended the one God through his own intellect and followed "the true way" also draws attention to Maimonides' universalism: "He was submerged, in Ur of the Chaldees, among silly idolaters. His father and mother and the entire population worshipped idols, and he worshipped with them. But his mind was busily working and reflecting till he attained the way of truth, apprehended the correct line of thought and knew that there is One God, that He governs the celestial Sphere and created everything, and that among all that exist, there is no god beside Him. He realized that the whole world was in error...." *The Guide* further casts Abraham as the prototype of a universal monotheist-teacher: "Abraham our father was the first to make known the belief in unity, to establish prophecy, and to perpetuate this opinion and draw people to it." Abraham, Isaac, and Jacob "were perfect people in their opinions and in their moral character" and "the end of their efforts during their life was to bring into being a religious community that would know and worship God."

A related universalistic vision of every human being's potential "to know God" is rendered in the concluding flourish of the *Mishneh Torah's Book of Agriculture* marking the mid-point of the *Mishneh Torah's* fourteen books: "Not only the Tribe of Levi, but also each and every individual of those who come into the world, whose spirit moves him and whose knowledge gives him understanding to set himself apart in order to stand before the Lord, to serve Him, to worship Him, and to know Him, who walks upright as God had made him to do, and releases his neck from the many speculations that the children of man are wont to pursue—such an individual is consecrated to the Holy of Holies, and his portion and inheritance shall be the Lord forever and evermore...." Accordingly, every human being is created "in the image of God" with the capacity to attain knowledge of God and through virtuous behavior, serving, worshipping, and knowing God reach holiness. The Torah provides the Jews with an impeccable blueprint for doing so and thereby achieving moral perfection. For those who have reached moral perfection, the sole limitation on seeking and accomplishing "human perfection" is the capability of an individual (Jew or gentile) to transform the "potential intellect" into a fully realized "acquired intellect," as set forth in *The Guide's* exposition, "knowing everything concerning all beings that it is within the capacity of man to know in accordance with his ultimate perfection." To put it in the preferred terms of the *Commentary on the Mishnah* and the *Mishneh Torah*: the righteous, Jew and gentile alike, "have a portion in the world to come."

Did Maimonides' humanistic historicism extend to Christianity and Islam? It depends on where we look in the Maimonidean corpus. *The Guide of the Perplexed* observes the common ground between the three religious traditions: "There is no doubt that there are things that are common to all three of us, I mean the Jews, the Christians, and the Muslims: namely, the affirmation of the temporal creation of the world, the validity of which entails the validity of miracles and other things of that kind." The *Epistle to Yemen*, by contrast, is tailored to respond to the specific historical crisis engulfing its audience. The *Epistle* levels an uncompromising polemic against Christianity and especially Islamdom, the political structure in which Muslims are sovereign. In the context of presenting a capsule history of monotheism, the final chapters of *Mishneh Torah* answer the question quite differently. Christianity and Islam acknowledge the Torah (more or less), but they decry the authentic truth of Torah as the Jews read, understand, and observe it. The *Mishneh Torah*'s halakhic rulings view Christianity as a secondary form of idolatry, that is, worship of God through Jesus as an intermediary.

As for Islam, Maimonides deviated from the opinions of his geonic predecessors. Maimonides was adamant that Islam was purely monotheistic, and he asserted this judgment on multiple occasions. The *Mishneh Torah* illustrates several ways in which "The Law," as Maimonides understood it, assigns Muslims a halakhic category somewhat distinct from that of Christians. *The Code* tells us that the practice of circumcision became an obligation for Muslims in addition to the seven Noahide laws: "The Rabbis said that the sons of Keturah, who are of the seed of Abraham and who were born after Ishmael and Isaac, are bound to observe the precept of circumcision. Since today the descendants of Ishmael are intermingled with the descendants of Keturah, they are bound to observe the rite of circumcision on the eighth day...." A halakhic ruling regarding forbidden wine explicitly identifies Muslims as gentiles "who do not worship idols," contrary to Christians. Maimonides' legal opinions also accommodated Jewish business partnerships with Muslims in Islamdom.

The soaring conclusion of the *Mishneh Torah* in the final chapters of *The Book of Judges* adopts a historical perspective on the function of the global compass of Christianity and Islam. Chapter 11, "Kings and War," refers to Jesus in polemical fashion. This text was censored by the Church during the Middle Ages but fortunately survived in manuscript form. The critical passage condemns Jesus and Muhammad for their manufactured inventions and contrivances yet affords Christianity and Islam a crucial role in the divine design of history. In Maimonides' scheme their global diffusion weans the multitudes from pagan beliefs and practices in preparation for the messianic age and the universal monotheism that will mark the end of its process. "But it is beyond the human mind to fathom the designs of the Creator; for our ways are not His ways, neither our thoughts His thoughts. All these matters relating to Jesus of Nazareth and the Ishmaelite (Muhammad) who came after him, only served to clear the way for King Messiah, to prepare the whole world to worship God with one accord as it is written 'For then will I turn to the peoples a pure language, that they may all call upon the name of the Lord to serve Him with one consent' (Zeph. 3:9). Thus the messianic hope, the Torah, and the commandments have become familiar topics—topics of conversation (among the inhabitants) of the far isles and many peoples, uncircumcised of heart and flesh…."

Perhaps Maimonides always conceived of Christianity (along with Islam) as unwittingly fulfilling the historic mission charted here—"to prepare the whole world to worship God with one accord" by introducing, incorporating, and disseminating the Torah's essential ideas—or alternatively his thinking about Christianity evolved toward the more universalistic view over the course of writing and revising *The Code*. In any case, the *Mishneh Torah* concludes with a prophetic vision dissolving the ultimate distinction between Jews and gentiles that will characterize the messianic age.

Chapter 6
Maimonides in historical perspective

Moses Maimonides has loomed large as spectral presence in Jewish life, culture, and thought throughout the eight centuries since he died. His letters, epistles, *responsa*, and books have been read, studied, interpreted, translated, and rewritten, such that Maimonides has been recast and reinvented many times over. Writers, thinkers, and communal leaders have drawn upon Maimonides' intellectual charisma and the authority it confers for purposes he scarcely imagined. Today, Maimonides' name graces medical centers, hospitals, and educational institutions in the United States, Israel, and Europe.

Maimonides remains the subject of fascination, inspiration, and source of authority in many domains of Jewish experience. The 800th anniversary of Maimonides' death in 2004 produced numerous scholarly and popular publications, symposia, colloquia, exhibits, and other commemorations. His widely disseminated works, influential in every sphere of his intellectual and literary activity, remain the objects of traditional and academic study in their original languages and in translation. A database search through the Cornell University Library results in 20,400 Maimonides-related items listed in libraries worldwide. The true number of publications dedicated to him is arguably even larger.

Throughout the Sephardi Jewish diaspora and among the Jews of Middle Eastern lands heroic folktales on Maimonides abound. He was especially beloved by the Jews of Yemen who frequently identified him in their literature as "Moses of our time." The thirteenth-century Catalonian scholar Moses ben Naḥman (Nahmanides), who respected Maimonides for his unequaled command of rabbinic learning but criticized him for his innovations and philosophical directives, reported that the Jews of Yemen inserted Maimonides' name into their recitation of a canonical prayer, the Kaddish, which appears multiple times in every synagogue service and on other liturgical occasions: "In your lifetime and during your days and during the life of Rabbi Moses ben Maimon."

Abraham Maimonides, Maimonides' only child, served as the immediate and principal guardian of his father's rabbinic and philosophical intellectual legacy. A religious intellectual, physician, scientist, communal authority, and major figure in his own right among the Jews of Egypt, he championed the "Great Rav in Israel's" work and defended his reputation. Abraham viewed his father as a model to emulate even while charting his own pietistic course or harmonizing Moses' philosophically minded biblical exegesis with other approaches. S. D. Goitein devoted an entire subchapter of his magisterial study of the documents of the Cairo Geniza to Abraham. He deemed him "a paradigm of learned orthodoxy" devoted to upholding his father's teaching.

Like Abraham, Maimonides' followers played a critical role in preserving his memory, works, and ideas. Samuel ibn Tibbon's authoritative translation of *The Guide of the Perplexed* into Hebrew first appeared in 1204 and was revised in 1213 with an accompanying glossary of the philosophical terms he invented for the purpose. He also composed *Explanation of Unfamiliar Terms*, the first Hebrew philosophical lexicon as a study aid.

Samuel's *Commentary on Ecclesiastes*, one of the Hebrew Bible's books devoted to wisdom, was inspired by and hews closely to Maimonides' interpretive method. The *Commentary*'s preface proclaims the disciple's dedication to his master: "Everything I interpret in it [this commentary] concerning wisdom, I interpret only in accordance with what is revealed to me in his books, according to what his opinion is in these matters. For I partake from his waters and make others imbibe [BT Hagigah 3a–b]. Everything comes from the fruit of the righteous and his good work which is life itself and causes life, continuously and forever."

Ibn Tibbon's Hebrew translation of *The Guide* made the work available to Jewish intellectuals in the Christian Iberian kingdoms and especially for a group of Maimonides' followers in Provence. These students afforded Maimonides very high hopes for the future of advanced study of the Torah as he taught it, that is, as imbued with philosophy. Among Moses' devotees during his lifetime and immediately thereafter, Judah al-Harizi was also noteworthy. Al-Harizi's Hebrew rendition of *The Guide* was at once more readable, literary, and authentically Hebraic than Ibn Tibbon's technical, philosophically minded translation. During his journey to the Islamic East, al-Harizi met Abraham Maimonides. He paid poetic tribute to Abraham as his august father's worthy successor in the poem of praise dedicated to the deceased Maimonides:

> He [Moses] bequeathed his glorious attire to his son;
> How fair is the adorned, and how comely the garment!...
> One master passed on, leaving another as heir.
> One light subsided, but another emerged.
> When the one vanished the other appears.

Tanhum ben Joseph ha-Yerushalmi, a Maimonidean Egyptian Jewish literary and religious intellectual, composed *The Sufficient Guide*, a glossary of difficult words in the *Mishneh Torah*.

To enhance use of *The Code* and resituate it in rabbinic tradition, other scholars also endeavored to supply the *Mishneh Torah* with the rabbinic sources Maimonides omitted. Levi ben Gerson (Gersonides), a highly innovative Provencal philosopher, scholar of Jewish law, and biblical exegete, was arguably the most radical Maimonidean of all (while departing from Maimonides on occasion) in his complete dedication to science and reason as critical elements of an apparatus for reinterpreting Jewish tradition.

The Guide of the Perplexed generated scriptural-based sermons by figures such as the physician and philosopher Jacob Anatoli (Ibn Tibbon's son-in-law and Frederick II's court translator of Arabic to Hebrew), and biblical exegesis by Anatoli's son Moses, Menahem ha-Me'iri, the distinguished rabbinic scholar, and the poet and bellelettrist Immanuel ben Solomon of Rome. *The Guide* was also the subject of Hebrew commentaries each with its own focus and method, based primarily on Ibn Tibbon's translation. The Iberian, Provencal, and Italian commentators on *The Guide* included important figures in Jewish intellectual life. To name a few of the most prominent: the scholar and polemicist Moses ben Solomon of Salerno; Shem Tov ben Joseph ibn Falaquera, a Hebrew poet, philosopher, and author of one of the first Hebrew encyclopedias of science and philosophy; the grammarian, exegete, and thinker Joseph ibn Kaspi; the philosopher and physician Moses Narboni; Profayt Duran (also known as ha-Efodi and by his converso name Maestre Honoratus de Bonafide), a Hebrew grammarian, astronomer, philosopher, and astrologer to the Aragonese court; and David ben Messer Leon, a Renaissance rabbi and philosopher. Even authors in early modern Ashkenaz down to the Jewish Enlightenment thinker Solomon Maimon were drawn to compose commentaries on *The Guide*.

The earliest complete Latin translation of *The Guide*, an anonymous work of unknown provenance from the mid-thirteenth century, is based largely on al-Harizi's Hebrew version. This work and other partial and full translations rendered Maimonides' thought accessible to Christian scholastics such as Thomas Aquinas who refers to him respectfully and draws upon his work but opposed his approach to specific questions. Aquinas exploits Maimonides' deft exposure of the problematic limitations of human language in discussion of God's "names." But he sharply disagrees with Maimonides' totalizing application of "negative attributes" and with his positions on whether the world began in time or is eternal, the nature of God's knowledge, and God's foreknowledge of human actions, that is, the meaning of "free will." In the sixteenth century, *The Guide* was of such interest that it was translated into vernacular Spanish and Italian based on Ibn Tibbon's Hebrew text. The Latin and vulgar translations secured Maimonides a prominent place in the wider sphere of medieval and early modern Christian religious thought including figures such as Albert the Great and Meister Eckhart.

The opposition and discord Maimonides confronted during his lifetime erupted into the full blown "Maimonidean controversy" of the thirteenth century. A Catholic heresy with an allegorical interpretation of Scripture, the rise of early universities as centers of alternate learning and authority, and the church's response to both challenges perhaps served as the background and context for the storm between Jewish religious intellectuals of contending orientations. Early in the century Solomon ben Abraham of Montpellier and his disciples expressed alarm at the trend among Maimonideans to interpret philosophically the Hebrew Bible and rabbinic midrash. Solomon and others sought unsuccessfully to ban *The Guide* and the *Book of Knowledge* and philosophy itself for ostensibly subverting the Torah. At its zenith, the "Maimonidean Controversy" principally involved apprehension regarding Maimonides' orthodoxy (as opposed to his manifest orthopraxy) based on anxiety over *The Guide*, opposition to *The Book of Knowledge* in the *Mishneh Torah*—after all a halakhic work—and suspicions regarding Moses' true philosophical orientation. Centered in the Christian Iberian kingdoms and Provence, the controversy was so intense that Solomon persuaded the rabbis of France to ban *The Guide* and *The Book of Knowledge*. These books purportedly were burned in public in Montpellier in 1232, allegedly because Jews hostile to Maimonides' thinking denounced his works to the Church. The Aragonese sage Nahmanides endeavored ineffectively to quell the intercommunal strife. In 1305 Rabbi Solomon ibn Adret of Barcelona promulgated a ban on studying philosophy and science until the age of twenty-five, in the controversy's culminating episode. The imbroglio between rationalists and anti-rationalists over the legitimacy of science and philosophy came to dominate much of Jewish intellectual life in Christian Iberia through the fourteenth century in a fraught struggle between proponents of rival cultural ecosystems compounded by social tensions between aristocrats and Talmudists. *The Guide* also met with opposition from pietist circles in Egypt, even among those otherwise close to Abraham Maimonides. Distant echoes of the Maimonidean Controversy survive in traditionalist circles today, although much of the disagreement reflects what is imagined, invented, and misunderstood rather than what is comprehended and fathomed, as was the case in the thirteenth century. Opponents of Maimonides' ethos knew (and know) enough to understand they had to reckon with his imposing reputation, momentous body of work, and its enthusiastic reception in many quarters.

Maimonideans rose to the challenge through the decades. Amid reports that *The Guide* was burned in Montpellier, Abraham Maimonides joined the controversy. He dedicated a book entitled *Wars of the Lord* to championing his father's teachings on divine incorporeality and other contested matters. For his part al-Harizi defended Maimonides, "of the saints of God," in glowing rhymed prose and poetry, denouncing his critics and would-be rivals for their envy and gross error of their ways in rhetorically charged expressions: "Yet there arose in his wake a faction, whose attainment of knowledge was a fraction. On account of their trivial learning and slight understanding against his writings took action, and through their ignorance of his greatness attacked his compositions in order to extinguish the light of his vision.... For the custom of these folk of slight intelligence, who forsake the sciences, who recognize not virtue of the virtuous and deem that naught exist beside them, and all their aim and purpose is to malign God's saints.... The rank of these folks in regards to him is that of a falcon in comparison to an eagle. Their knowledge compared to him is as a brook unto the seven seas, and their worth aside his—a lantern against the moon!"

David Qimhi, a Provencal biblical commentator from a distinguished Andalusi scholarly background, joined the fray in a polemical, epistolary exchange with Jonah ben Abraham Gerondi, a follower of Solomon ben Abraham. Shem Tov ibn Falaquera also engaged in a futile literary effort to persuade staunch anti-rationalist anti-Maimonideans of the religious benefit of studying *The Guide* and philosophy and science more generally. Toward the demise of Jewish life in Iberia, the scholar, biblical commentator, thinker, and courtier Don Isaac Abravanel composed the most comprehensive commentary on Maimonides' *Thirteen Principles*. Abravanel defended Maimonides and his formulations (albeit with critical ambivalence: "this is the intention of our master Moses [Maimonides] but not the intention of Moses our master") against Hasdai Crescas and his student Joseph Albo, two of Maimonides' most important and severe late medieval detractors.

Notwithstanding the controversy and the residual anti-philosophical sensibility in Iberian Jewish culture, Maimonides' thought resurfaced and secured an exceptional place in early modern and modern Jewish intellectual history. His impact is reflected in the works of such important and diverse enlightenment figures as the philosophers Baruch (Benedict) Spinoza, Moses Mendelsohn, Nahman Krochmal (author of the *Guide for the Perplexed of Our Time*), and the neo-Kantian Hermann Cohen. Each scholar deeply engaged and appropriated aspects of

Maimonides' thought in crafting their own ethical, political, intellectual, and theological visions.

In our own time David Hartman (*Israelis and the Jewish Tradition: An Ancient People Debating its Future*, 2000), Micah Goodman (*Maimonides and the Book That Changed Judaism: Secrets of The Guide for the Perplexed*, 2015), and James Diamond and Menachem Kellner (*Reinventing Maimonides in Contemporary Jewish Thought*, 2019) are among many Jewish intellectuals to write books devoted to bringing into the public square Maimonides' thought and awareness of the transformations it has undergone to serve various purposes beyond his own. For that matter Maimonides' reputation as a healer has inspired books offering his medical advice to modern society avid for all manner of restorative and therapeutic guidance (for instance, *The Life Transforming Diet: Based on Health and Psychological Principles of Maimonides*, 2013; *The Health Directives of Maimonides*, 2015).

Maimonides, or indications to his work, appears as a character or referent in literary texts as well. *Latent Secret: Maimonides and his Friend Ibn Rushd* (2002) by Illy Gorlitzki, is a Hebrew novel about Maimonides' imagined friendship and correspondence with his Andalusi Muslim compatriot. *Maimonides and Spinoza Come to Dinner: A Hypothetical Conversation* (2018) by Juan Marcos Bejarano Gutierrez pits the two great thinkers in fictional dialogue. For her part the writer and critic-turned-community activist Dara Horn authored *Guide for the Perplexed* (2013), a richly imagined novel which takes the reader on a transhistorical quest involving Maimonides, the Cairo Geniza, the first Geniza scholar Solomon Schechter, and the digital revolution. The heroic Maimonides even turns up as a figure in popular culture in modes and media he could never have imagined. *Rambam: The Story of Maimonides* is an animated documentary film and the official film of the Maimonides 800th Anniversary Festival voiced by Leonard Nimoy of *Star Trek* fame. *Rambam: The Story of Maimonides*

(English and French edition; 2006) relates his life story in the form of a graphic novel presumably to enlighten a younger and hip generation. The three-part documentary *In Search of Maimonides: The Great Eagle* (2022), directed by Uri Rosenwachs, also presents Maimonides' story and bearing in history.

10. A relief carving of Maimonides as imagined by the artist Brenda Putnam (1950) adorns the chamber of the House of Representatives in the U.S. Capitol, one of twenty-three great lawgivers in history so designated.

Given Maimonides' commanding impact on centuries of Jewish life and culture, it is no wonder that the epitaph on his tomb in Tiberias captures his transcendent stature. It is inscribed with a traditional adage of exceptional homage: "From Moses to Moses, there was none like Moses."

References

Abbreviations

BC Moses Maimonides, *Mishneh Torah: The Book of Commandments* [Hebrew]. Two volumes. Translated by Shraga Silverstein. New York and Jerusalem: Moznaim Publishing, 1993.

BT Babylonian Talmud

CM Qafih Moses Maimonides, *Commentary on the Mishnah* [Hebrew]. Three volumes. Translated by Joseph Qafih. Jerusalem: Mossad Harav Kook, 1975.

CM Twersky Moses Maimonides, *Commentary on the Mishnah*. Translated excerpts in Isadore Twersky, *A Maimonides Reader*. Springfield, NJ: Behrman House, 1972.

EC Moses Maimonides, *The Eight Chapters* (*Maimonides on Ethics*). Translated by Raymond L. Weiss and Charles Butterworth in *Ethical Writings of Maimonides*. New York: Dover, 1983. 59–104.

EM Moses Maimonides, *Epistle on Martyrdom*. Translated by Abraham Halkin, in *Epistles of Maimonides: Crisis and Leadership*, Abraham Halkin and David Hartman. Philadelphia: Jewish Publication Society, 1985. 15–33.

EY Moses Maimonides, *The Epistle to Yemen*. Translated by Joel L. Kraemer, in *Maimonides' Empire of Light: Popular Enlightenment in an Age of Belief.* Ed. Ralph Lerner. Chicago and London: University of Chicago Press, 2000. 99–132.

GP Moses Maimonides, *The Guide of the Perplexed*. Two volumes. Translated with an Introduction and Notes by Shlomo Pines. Introductory Essay by Leo Strauss. Chicago: University of Chicago Press, 1963. References to *The Guide* in this book refer to Part and Chapter, followed by volume and page in brackets.

LA Moses Maimonides, *Epistle on Astrology*. Translated by Ralph Lerner in *Maimonides' Empire of Light: Popular Enlightenment in an Age of Belief*. Ed. Ralph Lerner. Chicago and London: University of Chicago Press, 2000. 178–87.

LC Maimon ben Joseph, *Letter of Consolation*. Translated by Fred Rosner. Haifa: Maimonides Research Institute, 2003.

LM Moses Maimonides, *Letters of Maimonides* [Arabic and Hebrew]. Third revised edition. Two volumes in one. Ed. Isaac Shailat. Maaleh Adumim: Maaliyot Press, 1995.

MA *The Medical Aphorisms of Moses Maimonides* (*Maimonides Medical Writings*). Translated and annotated by Fred Rosner with bibliography by Jacob I. Dienstag. Haifa: The Maimonides Research Institute, 1989.

MR Moses Maimonides, *T'shuvot ha-rambam* (*Maimonides' Responsa*) [Hebrew and Arabic]. Four volumes. Ed. Joshua Blau. Jerusalem: Rubin Mass, 2014.

MT-BA Moses Maimonides, *The Code of Maimonides: The Book of Agriculture*. Translated by Isaac Klein. New Haven and London: Yale University Press, 1979.

MT-BH Moses Maimonides, *The Code of Maimonides: The Book of Holiness*. Translated by Louis I. Rabinowitz and Philip Grossman. New Haven: Yale University Press, 1965.

MT-BJ Moses Maimonides, *The Code of Maimonides, Book Fourteen: [Mishneh Torah] The Book of Judges*. Translated by Abraham Hershman. New Haven: Yale University Press, 1949.

MT-BK Lerner Moses Maimonides, *Mishneh Torah*: Introduction and *The Book of Knowledge*. Translated by Ralph Lerner, in *Maimonides' Empire of Light: Popular Enlightenment in an Age of Belief*. Ed. Ralph Lerner. Chicago and London: University of Chicago Press, 2000. 133–53.

MT-BK Hyamson Moses Maimonides, *Mishneh Torah: The Book of Knowledge*. Edited with Introduction, Biblical and Talmudic References, Notes and English Translation by Moses Hyamson. New Corrected Edition. Jerusalem and New York: Feldheim, 1981.

MT-BL Moses Maimonides, *The Code of Maimonides: The Book of Love*. Translated by Menachem Marc Kellner. New Haven: Yale University Press, 2004.

TL "Moses Maimonides' Treatise on Logic (*Maḳāla fī ṣinā'at al-manṭiḳ*): The Original Arabic and Three Hebrew Translations." Edited and translated by Israel Efros in *Proceedings of the American Academy for Jewish Research* 8 (1937–39): 1–136.

TR Moses Maimonides, *Treatise on Resurrection*. Translated by
Hillel G. Fradkin, in *Maimonides' Empire of Light: Popular
Enlightenment in an Age of Belief*. Ed. Ralph Lerner. Chicago and
London: University of Chicago Press, 2000. 154–77.

Works by others

Constable, Olivia Remie, ed. *Medieval Iberia: Readings from
Christian, Muslim, and Jewish Sources*. Second edition.
Philadelphia: University of Pennsylvania Press, 2012.

Halkin, A. S. "Ibn 'Aknin's Commentary on the Song of Songs,"
in *Alexander Marx Jubilee Volume* [English Section].
Ed. Saul Lieberman. Philadelphia: Jewish Theological Seminary
of America, 1950. 389–434.

Ibn Abi 'Usaybi'ah. *A Literary History of Medicine: The 'Uyun
al-anba' fi tabaqat al-atibba' of Ibn Abi 'Usaybi'ah* (five volumes).
Ed. Emily Savage-Smith, Simon Swain, and Geert Jan van Gelder.
Leiden: Brill, 2020. Volume 3–2, 1247.

Ibn Sana' l-Mulk, Hibbat Allah ibn Ja'far. *Diwan*. [al-Maktaba
al-'arabiyya 75]. Ed. Muhammad Ibrahim Nasr. Cairo: Dar al-kitab
al-'arabi, 1969.

Judah al-Harizi, *Kitab al-Durar: A Book in Praise of God and the
Israelite Communities* [Arabic and Hebrew]. Assembled and
edited by Joshua Blau, Paul Fenton, and Joseph Yahalom.
Jerusalem: Ben-Zvi Institute for the Study of Jewish Communities
in the East and the Hebrew University, 2009.

Samuel ben Judah ibn Tibbon. *Commentary on Ecclesiastes (The Book
of the Soul of Man)* [Hebrew]. Edited with Introduction and Notes
by James T. Robinson. Jerusalem: World Union of Jewish
Studies, 2016.

> This book relies upon and cites published translations listed here
> or found in "For Further Reading" to enable the interested reader
> to follow up. References to and translations from Maimonides
> direct the reader to the texts above. Translated passages of primary
> texts appearing without citing a published translation are my own.

Introduction

"Realizing this amazing matter": *EM*, 24.
"the improvement of the moral qualities": *EC*, 38 [*Avot* 1].
"He was named Musa": al-Harizi, 76–77*.

Chapter 1: Maimonides and his world

"well informed regarding the issue": *EM*, 15.

"What I counsel myself": *EM*, 31.

"But in this persecution": *EM*, 20.

"This compulsion imposes": *EM*, 30.

"When I was your age": *LM*, 421.

"period of forcible conversion": Halkin 1950 (Ibn 'Aqnin), 403–4.

"They merely expressed": *EY*, 101.

"His eminent dignity": Kraemer 1991: 86–87.

"I think Galen's medical care": Ibn Sana' l-Mulk, 296.

"Al-Ra'is Musa (Master Musa) was Abu 'Imran Musa ibn Maymun
al-Qurtubī, a Jew": Ibn Abi 'Usaybi'ah 1247.

"I must tell you": *LM*, 299; 313.

"The worst disaster that struck me": Kraemer 2002: 424–45.

"I have seen fit": "Introduction to the *Mishneh Torah*," *MT-BK*
Lerner, 140.

"When I consider": Kraemer 2001: 427.

"Isn't he called by the name 'Moses'": *MR* 3:49–54.

Maimonides' reply in kind: *LM*, 499–510.

What is certain is that for Maimonides: *MT-BJ*, "Laws of Kings" 12:5.

"A mortal of the divine saints": al-Harizi, 71–77*.

Chapter 2: "Back home in the west"

"I am Moses ben Maimon, the Sefardi": *CM* Qafih, 1 [Hebrew
Introduction]; *LA*, 178.

"I am one of the least of the sages of Sefarad": *LY*, 2 [Hebrew
Introduction].

"As for the Andalusians among the people of our nation": *GP* 1:71 [1:177].

"Then came latter day groups of people in Andalusia": *GP* 2:9 [2:268].

"in clear language and succinctly": *MT-BK* Lerner, 140 [Introduction].

"and as for the Arabic and Hebrew languages": *LM*, 150.

"Regarding the Arabic and Hebrew vernaculars": *MA*, 431 [ch.
26 #58].

"The first purpose of this Treatise": *GP* 1:5–6 [Introduction to the
First Part].

"the manner of our fellows in the past": *LM*, 501.

Maimonides also repeated a rabbinic source reckoning study of the
"holy tongue": *CM* Qafih, *Avot* 2:1 [275].

"I composed *The Code* in it [Hebrew]": *LM*, 304.

languages, including Hebrew, originate by human convention: *GP* 2:30 [2:357–58].

the relative absence of sexual and execratory expressions: *GP* 3:8 [2:435–36].

are the most pleasant: *MA*, 429–31 [Treatise 25, aphorisms 56–58].

"The books of Aristotle": *LM*, 552–54.

"It is by necessity of reason": Constable, 246, 248.

"Excessive troubles and distressful times": *MT* [Introduction] Lerner, 139–40.

"Know that I have not composed this compendium": *LM*, 228–30; Kraemer 2001: 425.

"Torah from Heaven": *CM Pereq Heleq* in Kraemer 2008: 140.

"After having completed our previous well-known work": Twersky 1972: 425–26.

Chapter 3: Loving God with the mind

"Rationality we call man's difference": *TL*, 51–52.

"this intellect is not a faculty in the body": *GP* 1:72 [1:193].

"heed the truth, whoever may have said it": *CM Avot* ["Eight Chapters"] Introduction, 6.

"leads to great perfection": *CM Avot* ["Eight Chapters"], 34; Twersky 1972: 362.

"Know, my masters, that it is not proper": *LA*, 179.

"the apprehension of God": *EC*, 5:164/75–76.

"God, may His mention be exalted": *GP* 1 Introduction [1:8–9].

"there is no eating, drinking, washing": BT Berakhot 17a.

"I must now speak of the great fundamental principles": *CM* Twersky 1972: 402–23.

that herald the complete felicity: *MT-BK* Hyamson, "Laws of Repentance," 90a–93a [Chapters 8–10].

serves as a preparatory bridge or introduction: *BC* 1:101–4.

"Excessive troubles and distressful times": *MT-BK* [Introduction] Lerner, 139–40.

"The precept relating to idolatry": *MT-BK* [2:4] Hyamson, "Laws of Idolatry," 67b–68a.

The only virtue worth striving for: *GP* 3:54 [2:635].

"His commandments, His injunctions": *BC* positive commandment 3; Twersky 1972: 432.

"This honored and feared deity": *MT-BK* 2:12; Lerner, "Basic Principles of the Torah," 144.

"One only loves God": *MT-BK* [10:6] Hyamson, "Laws of Repentance"; Twersky 1972: 85.

"When a man reflects on these things": *MT-BK* 4:12; Lerner, 152.

"We have already explained": *GP* 3:28 [2:512–13].

"Know that the many sciences": *GP* 1:71 [1:175–76].

"The foundation of the foundations": *MT-BK* Lerner, 141–42.

"Know that the great foundation": *CM* Qafih *Pereq Heleq* [Sanhedrin 10:142].

"I have already made it known to you": *GP* 2:30 [2:349].

and in the *Mishneh Torah*: *MT-BK*, "Laws of Repentance" 3:6.

between "true beliefs" and "beliefs that are necessary": *GP* 3:28 [2:512].

"Thus we have mentioned there": *GP* 1 introduction [1:6–7].

The Guide's Introduction delineates seven causes: *GP* 1, Introduction: "Instruction with Respect to this Treatise" [1:17–18].

"very obscure parables occurring in the books of the prophets": *GP* 1, "Introduction to the First Part" [1:5–6].

"For my purpose is that the truths be glimpsed": *GP* 1, "Introduction to the First Part" [1:6–7].

"The term image": *GP* 1:1 [1:21–22].

"As for the term likeness": *GP* 1:1 [1:22–23].

"all these expressions and their like": *MT-BK* 1:9 Lerner, 143.

"You know their dictum": *GP* 1:26 [1:56].

"For there is no oneness at all except in believing": *GP* 1:51 [1:113].

"With regard to those three groups of attributes": *GP* 1:52 [1:116].

Only actions ascribed to God: *GP* 1:54 [1:128].

"Know that the description of God": *GP* 1:58 [1:134].

"conduct the mind toward the utmost reach": *GP* 1:58 [1:135].

"silence with regard to You is praise": *GP* 1:59 [1:139].

as the focus of a book Maimonides once began to write: *GP* 1: Introduction to the First Part [1:9].

"The sixth fundamental principle is prophecy": *CM* Twerksy 1972: 418–19; *CM* Qafih Sanhedrin 10:142.

"Know that the true reality and quiddity of prophecy": *GP* 2:36 [2:369].

"fully proficient in learning and completely accomplished in action": *CM* Qafih, 22–23.

"The Seventh Foundation is the prophecy of Moses": *CM* Qafih Sanhedrin 10:142; Twersky 1972: 419–20.

"His [Moses'] apprehension was not like that of the Patriarchs": *GP* 2:35 [2:367–68].

"After we have spoken of the quiddity of prophecy": *GP* 2:39
    [2:378–79].
only Moses attained a higher level of consciousness: *GP* 1:54 [1:125].
"Every commandment from these six hundred and thirteen": *GP* 3:31
    [2:524].
"For a sudden transition from one opposite to another": *GP* 3:32
    [2:526–28].
"I know that on thinking about this": *GP* 3:32 [2:527].
The cunning benevolence: Faur, 151–52.
"In the traditions of our prophets and those who transmit our Law":
    EC, 71–72.
"The Law as a whole aims at two things": *GP* 3:27 [2:510–11].
"Parable of the Palace": *GP* 3:51 [2:618].
the ruler's immediate presence: *GP* 3:51 [2:618–28].
"He, however, who has achieved demonstration": *GP* 3:51 [2:619].
"Know, my son . . . . If, however": *GP* 3:51 [2:619].
"Among them there is he who because of the greatness": *GP* 3:51 [2:620].
"It is clear that the perfection of man": *GP* 3:54 [2:638].

Chapter 4: The humanistic rabbi, philosopher, physician

"Thus it is clear that after apprehension": *GP* 3:51 [2:621].
"It is clear that the perfection of man": *GP* 3:54 [2:638].
Maimonides outlined the individual's self-governance: *TL*, 160–61.
"And were it not for the Torah, which is my delight": Kraemer
    2008: 255–56.
"The Creator of the world knows": Kraemer 2008: 440–41.
"occupying yourself in the true study of the Torah": *LM*, 298, 312.
"God sent Moses the prophet": al-Harizi, 76–77*.
"the study of medicine has a very great influence": *EC* [*CM* Avot], 70.
"walk in God's ways": *MT-BK* Hyamson 47b–48a.
"The sick in body taste what is bitter as sweet": *MT-BK*
    Hyamson 48a.
"No disciple of the wise may live in a city": *MT-BK* Hyamson 50a–52b.
"It is forbidden to lead the community": *MT-BJ*, 75 [Sanhedrin
    25:1–2].
"whoever adopts Judaism and confesses the unity": Twersky
    1972: 475–76.
"When your teacher called you a fool": *LM*, 238–41; Twersky
    1972: 477.

"First of all, I must tell you": Twersky 1972: 479.

"To the honored, great, and holy master and teacher": *EY*, 99.

"I have seen fit to write the response": *EY*, 101.

"Now then, O our brethren": *EY*, 108–9.

"I would request that you send": *EY*, 132.

"So rely upon these true texts": *EY*, 108.

"Never has a nation arisen against Israel": *EY*, 128.

"The precise time is unknowable": *EY*, 124.

"God is the best knower of the truth": *EY*, 125.

"Know, o thou man of speculation": *TR*, 162.

"reward or honor from human beings": *TR*, 155.

"The world to come is the reward": *TR*, 157.

Chapter 5: Turning the parochial into the universal

ordained for all of humankind to observe: *MT-BJ*, "Kings and Wars"
9:231–34.

"A heathen who accepts": *MT-BJ*, "Kings and Wars" 8:11 [230].

various forms of pagan idolatry: *MT-BK*, Hyamson and Qafih, "Laws
of Idolatry" 1:1.

educated his family and others: *MT-BK* Qafih, "Laws of Idolatry"
1:1–1:3; *GP* 2:30 [2:379].

divine "concession" for expressing their veneration: *GP* 3:32 [2:527].

"Do not think that in the days of the Messiah": *MT-BJ*, 240–41.

"The Sages and Prophets did not long for the days": *MT-BJ*, 242.

"This is—may God save us and you": *EY*, 102–3.

"He was submerged, in Ur of the Chaldees": *MT-BK* Qafih, "Laws of
Idolatry" 1:3; Hyamson 66b.

"Abraham our father was the first": *GP* 3:43 [2:572].

"were perfect people in their opinions": *GP* 3:51 [2:624].

"Not only the Tribe of Levi": *MT-BA*, "Laws of Sabbatical and Jubilee
Years" [13:13], 403.

"knowing everything concerning all beings": *GP* 3:27 [2:511].

"There is no doubt": *GP* 1:71 [1:178].

worship of God through Jesus as an intermediary: *MT-BK*, "Idolatry"
9:4 [76b].

"The Rabbis said that the sons of Keturah": *MT-BJ*, "Kings and their
Wars" [10:8], 236.

identifies Muslims as gentiles "who do not worship idols": *MT-BH*,
"Forbidden Foods" [11:7; 13:11] 209; 222.

"But it is beyond the human mind": *MT-BJ*, Introduction, xxii.

Chapter 6: Maimonides in historical perspective

"Everything I interpret": Ibn Tibbon, 86.
"He [Moses] bequeathed his glorious attire to his son": al-Harizi, 77*.
"Yet there arose in his wake a faction": al-Harizi, 71; 73*.

Further reading

Bos, Gerrit. *The Medical Works of Moses Maimonides*. Salt Lake City: Brigham Young University Press [Volumes 1–10], and Boston and Leiden: Brill, 2018– [Volumes 11–].

> This series presents critical editions of all of Maimonides' medical works with English translations. Seventeen volumes have appeared to date including, most recently, Maimonides' commentary on Hippocrates' *Aphorisms*.

Brody, Robert. *The Geonim of Babylonia and the Shaping of Medieval Jewish Culture*. New Haven, CT, and London: Yale University Press, 1998.

> Provides the Eastern Geonic background to developments in Jewish thought and rabbinic literary activity during the period before Maimonides.

Davidson, Herbert A. *Moses Maimonides, The Man and His Works*. Oxford: Oxford University Press, 2005.

> Offers a thorough overview of Maimonides' life and works. Affirms the essential unity of Maimonides' rabbinic and scientific-philosophical thinking.

Fauer, José. *Homo Mysticus: A Guide to Maimonides' Guide for the Perplexed*. Syracuse: Syracuse University Press, 1999.

> A completely original post-structural rereading of *The Guide* as a foundational text for Jewish philosophy.

Gillis, David. *Reading Maimonides' Mishneh Torah*. Oxford and Portland: Littman Library of Jewish Civilization, 2015.

> An innovative examination of *The Code* and Maimonides' understanding of the significance of Jewish law as designed to

bring order to the individual and society in accordance with cosmic harmony.

Goitein, S. D. *A Mediterranean Society: The Jewish Communities of the Arab World as Portrayed in the Documents of the Cairo Geniza.* Six volumes. Berkeley and Los Angeles: University of California Press, 1967–93.

Indispensable study of the documentary texts from the Cairo Geniza providing details of the society and culture Maimonides inhabited.

Halbertal, Moshe. *Maimonides: Life and Thought.* Princeton, NJ: Princeton University Press, 2014.

Demonstrates how Maimonides' work on the *Commentary on the Mishnah* and the *Book of Commandments* prepared the way for his monumental undertaking in the *Mishneh Torah.*

Halkin, A. S. *Epistles of Maimonides: Crisis and Leadership.* Philadelphia: Jewish Publication Society, 1993.

Translation, commentary, and study of three of Maimonides' most important epistles.

Harvey, Steven. "Maimonides in the Sultan's Palace," in *Perspectives on Maimonides.* Philosophical and Historical Studies. Ed. Joel L. Kraemer. Oxford: Littman Library of Jewish Civilization, 1991. 47–75.

Keen analysis of Maimonides' famous parable in Book Three of *The Guide of the Perplexed.*

Ivry, Alfred L. *Maimonides' Guide of the Perplexed: A Philosophical Guide.* Chicago and London: University of Chicago Press, 2016.

A definitive guide to reading and studying *The Guide*'s content, and the interplay between its opaque and transparent styles.

Kellner, Menachem. *Science in the Bet Midrash: Studies in Maimonides.* Boston: Academic Studies Press, 2009.

The prolific author is one of the foremost interpreters of Maimonides' dual devotion to Torah and philosophy. This collection of studies presents the distillation of Kellner's reading of what he refers to as Maimonides' "institutionalist and nominalist" Judaism.

Kellner, Menachem, and David Gilles. *Maimonides the Universalist.* Oxford: Littman Library of Jewish Civilization, 2020.

Essential reading expanding the horizons of Twersky's *Introduction to the Code of Maimonides' (Mishneh Torah).* Twersky provides all the technical details necessary to understand *The Code* while Kellner and Gillis provide an informed reading of the work and its significance.

Kraemer, Joel L. *Maimonides: The Life and World of One of Civilization's Greatest Minds*. New York: Doubleday, 2008.

> The most complete intellectual biography of Maimonides.

Kraemer, Joel L. "The Life of Moses ben Maimon," in *Judaism in Practice from the Middle Ages through the Early Modern Period*. Ed. Lawrence Fine. Princeton, NJ: Princeton University Press, 2001. 413–28.

> Translation of eleven important primary texts by or about Maimonides.

Kraemer, Joel L. "Six Unpublished Maimonides Letters from the Cairo Genizah," *Maimonidean Studies* 2 (1991): 61–94.

> The Cairo Geniza contained many private occasional texts on personal, economic, and legal matters about or by Maimonides including several autograph letters and notes.

Kreisel, Howard. *Maimonides' Political Thought: Studies in Ethics, Law, and the Human Ideal*. Albany: SUNY Press, 1988.

> An extremely important study of the ways in which Maimonides' political philosophy informs his understanding of the significance of Jewish law and the ultimate purpose of human life.

Leicht, Reimund. "A Maimonidean Life: Joseph ben Judah ibn Shim'on of Ceuta's Biography Reconstructed," *Maimonides Review of Philosophy and Religion* 1 (2020): 1–48.

> An up-to-date study of this important figure in Maimonides' life relying on published and Geniza materials.

Manekin, Charles H. *On Maimonides*. Belmont, CA: Thomson Wadsworth, 2005.

> A succinct and extremely valuable presentation of Maimonides' positions on the major philosophical issues of his time.

Moses Maimonides, *The Guide of the Perplexed*. Two volumes. Translated with an Introduction and Notes by Shlomo Pines. Introductory Essay by Leo Strauss. Chicago: University Chicago Press, 1963.

> Since its publication this work has served as the standard English translation of *The Guide*. Pines' and Strauss' introductory essays are controversial interpretations of *The Guide*. Pines' translation has also been criticized for its rendering of key terms and reliance on an Arabic original in need of updating. A new translation of *The Guide of the Perplexed* is forthcoming.

Stern, Josef. *The Matter and Form of Maimonides' Guide*. Cambridge, MA, and London: Harvard University Press, 2013.
>A penetrating philosophical study of *The Guide* providing a thorough skeptical analysis of Maimonides thought through attention to its sources.

Stillman, Norman A. [Editor]. *Encyclopedia of Jews in the Islamic World*. Five volumes. Leiden and Boston: Brill, 2010.
>Indispensable resource with bibliography for further study of all of the individual names, concepts, works and places mentioned in this book.

Stroumsa, Sarah. *Maimonides in His World*. Princeton, NJ: Princeton University Press, 2009.
>A pathbreaking study of Maimonides in his multiple intellectual contexts with special attention to the Almohad environment of his formative years.

Twerksy, Isadore. *Introduction to the Code of Maimonides (Mishneh Torah)*. New Haven, CT, and London: Yale University Press, 1980.
>The most complete study of the form and content of the *Mishneh Torah*.

Twerksy, Isadore. *A Maimonides Reader*. Springfield, NJ: Behrman House, 1972.
>A still excellent introduction to Maimonides through translations of his works along with brief introductions.

Chronology

1138	Maimonides born in Cordoba
1148	Almohad troops arrive in Cordoba; Maimonides' family begins years of relocating around al-Andalus
1157/8	Completes *Treatise on the Calendar*
1159/60	Maimonides' family moves to Almohad Fez
1160-65	Authors the *Epistle on Forced Conversion*
1165	Maimonides' family leaves Morocco and arrives in Acre; makes pilgrimage to Jerusalem
1166	Maimonides' family settles in Fustat (Old Cairo) under Fatimid rule
1167/68	Completes his *Commentary on the Mishnah*
1168-77	Works on the *Mishneh Torah*
ca. 1170	Maimon b. Joseph, Maimonides' father, dies
ca. 1170-71	Maimonides' brother, David, drowns in an Indian Ocean shipwreck
1171-72	Maimonides serves as "Head of the Jews" under Ayyubid rule
ca. 1173	Maimonides marries daughter of Egyptian Jewish dignitary and physician
1172	*Epistle to Yemen*
1185	Maimonides begins work on *The Guide*
1186	Abraham Maimonides is born

ca. 1191	Maimonides completes *The Guide*
1194–96	Exchange of letters with the rabbis of Provence
1198–99	Maimonides serves again as "Head of the Jews"
1199	Letter to Samuel ibn Tibbon about translating *The Guide*
1204	Maimonides dies in Cairo

Index

Note: Figures are indicated by an italic "*f*", respectively, following the page number.

A

Abbasids 37–8
'Abd al-Mu'min 11
Abraham (biblical) 87–8, 98–100, 102–3
Abraham ben David (Rabad) 92–3
Abravanel, Don Isaac 112
Abu Bakr Ibn al-Sa'igh 28–9
Abulafia, Meir Halevi (Ramah) 92–3
Abu Ya'qub Yusuf 11–12
adab 32–3
al-Afdal al-Malik 'Ali 19–20, 23–4
Albert the Great 109–10
Albo, Joseph 112
Alexander of Aphrodisias 40–1
Alfasi, Isaac ben Jacob 7–8
Alfonso VI 7
Almohad Creed (*al-'Aqida*) 41–3, 56
Almohads
  Andalusian rule 8–10, 31–2
  Berbers 7, 41–2, 91
  coerced conversions 8–13, 19–20
  crypto-Jews under 11, 13–15

  influence on Maimonides 41–3, 56
  Islamic law 48–9
  persecution of Jews 12–13, 89–90
  philosophical thought 41–3, 57–8
Almoravids 7–10
Anatoli, Jacob 109
Anatoli, Moses 109
al-Andalus
  Almohad rule in 8–10, 31–2
  Almoravid rule in 7–10
  Arabization of Jews 29–34
  collapse of 7
  crypto-Jews in 11, 19–20, 41–2
  ignorance of Torah 56
  Islamic thought in 30, 39–40
  Jewish community in 4, 7–8, 25–6, 56, 89–90
  Jewish scholars in 30–1, 39–40, 43, 46–9, 58–9
  Judeo-Arabic education 31–4
  Neoplatonism in 39–40
  Sephardi Jews 28–9
  Umayyad Andalusi emirate 6

Arabic
affinity with Hebrew 33–4
Andalusi idioms 28
Greek science and philosophy 38
Jewish intellectuals and 29–31
Maimonides use of 10, 21–2, 28, 30–1, 36
translation to Hebrew 25–6
Aramaic 33–4, 36–7, 88–9
Aristotle
Almohad Creed (*al-'Aqida*) influence 41–3
Andalusi tradition 31–2
ethical behavior and 84–5
humanism of 38
influence on Maimonides 1, 36–7, 40–1, 74
metaphysics 41–3, 56–7
Metaphysics 41–3
rabbinic Judaism and 39
sciences and 40–1, 50, 56–7
Ash'arite 39
Ashkenazi Jewish communities 1–2, 54–5, 109
astrology 50–1, 89–92
Ayyubids 17–20, 91

B

Bahya ibn Paquda 39–40, 56–8, 67–8
al-Balia, Isaac ben Barukh 43
Bejarano Gutierrez, Juan Marcos 113–14
Ben Ezra Synagogue 80–1*f*
Book of Healing, The (Ibn Sina) 83
Book of Laws (*Sefer ha-halakhot*) (al-Fasi) 44–5
Book of Tradition, The (ibn Daud) 31–2

C

Cairo Geniza 2, 8–10, 16–17, 80–3*f*, 85–7*f*

Castile 7, 10, 31–2
Catholicism 8–10
Christianity
Almoravids rule 7
Andalusia 8–11
in Castile 10, 31–2
coerced conversions 8–10
Crusaders and 13–16, 24
Greek science and philosophy 37–8
idolatry and 103–4
as imitative religion 91
influence of Maimonides 109–10
in Islamdom 29–30
Maimonidean Controversy 110–11
Maimonides on 105
monotheism 105
rational theology 38–9
religious common ground 103–4
Cohen, Hermann 112–13
Commentary on Ecclesiastes (ibn Tibbon) 107–8
conversion
to Catholicism 8–10
crypto-Jews and 8–12, 19–20, 41–2
forced by Almohad rule 8–13, 41–2
Yemeni Jews 89–90
Cordoba, al-Andalus 6–10*f*
Crescas, Hasdai 112

D

David ben Messer Leon 109
Diamond, James 113
Divine Unity (*tawhid*) 35, 38–43
Dunash ben Tamim 39–40
Duran, Profayt 109

E

Eckhart, Meister 109–10

Egypt
  Ayyubids rule 17–19, 91
  Fatimids 18–19, 40, 91
  Jewish community in 15, 17–19,
    79–80, 93–4
  Maimon family in 15
  Maimonides influence in 1,
    15–16, 93–4, 110–11
  opposition to *Guide* 110–11
  tripartite Jewish community
    18–19
Explanation of Unfamiliar Terms
  (ibn Tibbon) 107–8

F

al-Farabi
  Attainment of Happiness
    70–1
  on divine attributes 67–8
  on languages 36–7
  Maimonides and 40–1
  on philosophy and religion
    51, 57–8
al-Fasi, Isaac 43–5
Fatimids 15, 18–19, 40, 91
Fez, Morocco
  Almohad 11–15
  Islamic civilization in 13–15*f*
  Jewish culture in 8–11, 30
  Maimon family in 11–15*f*
Fustat (Old Cairo) 2, 8–10, 15

G

Galen 36–7, 83
Geonim 43, 45–6, 55–6
al-Ghazali 42–3, 61–2
God
  anthropomorphic representations
    23, 35, 40–2, 53–4,
    60–1, 66–7
  biblical directive to love
    57–8, 60–1
  divine attributes 66–8

divine unity of 35, 38–43, 52–3,
    59–60, 66–7
  eternality of 61–2
  ethical behavior and 66–7
  human perfection and 76–7
  Jewish law and 22
  kalam (rational theology) 39
  knowledge of 53–4, 58–61
  theophany 70
Goitein, S. D. 107
Goodman, Micah 113
Gorlitzki, Illy 113–14
Great Mosque of Cordoba 7*f*
Great Rav in Israel 18–19
Greek science and philosophy
  Andalusi scholars 31–2
  humanism in 38
  Maimonides on 36–7,
    40–1, 58–9
  Muslim encounters with 37–8
  rabbinic Judaism 39
Guide for the Perplexed (Horn)
  113–14

H

halakha (Jewish law) *see* Jewish law
Hananel ben Hushiel 44–5
Hanokh ben Moses 43
al-Harizi, Judah
  defense of Maimonides 111–12
  translations to Hebrew 25–6,
    108–10
  tribute to Abraham Maimonides
    108
  tribute to Maimonides 5,
    25–7, 83
Hartman, David 113
Harun al-Rashid 37–8
Hayyuj, Judah 33–4
Head of the Jews 17–20
Hebrew Bible
  divine attributes 50–67
  equivocal terms 50–65
  Jewish principles 1–2, 54

Hebrew Bible (*Continued*)
Jewish scholarly production 30
Karaites 18–19
language of 34–5
literal interpretation of 18–19, 35, 64–5
philosophical perspective 110–11
prophecy in 69–70
Quranic exegesis 32–3
rabbinic Judaism 39
Hebrew language
affinity with Arabic and Aramaic 33–4
biblical exegesis 30, 32–5
exile-induced lost knowledge 58–9
Maimonides
appreciation of 35–7
rabbinic 31, 35–7
Torah laws in 54–6
written Judeo-Arabic 30–1
Hebrew poetry 31–2, 34–5
Horn, Dara 113–14
Hoter ben Solomon 54–5
Hrotsvit of Gandersheim 6
human perfection
in *Commentary* 51, 69–71, 74
in *Guide* 74–7, 79, 103
Hygiene of the Soul (Ibn 'Aqnin) 31–2

Iberia
Christian kingdoms in 7, 108, 110–11
demise of Jewish life in 112
Golden Age of Jewish culture in 6–7
Jewish scholars in 109–13
Ibn Abi Usaybi'a 19–20
ibn Adret, Solomon 110–11
Ibn al-Aflah 28–9
Ibn al-Qifti 19–20

ibn 'Aqnin, Joseph ben Judah 8–10, 12–13, 31–2
Ibn Bajja 40–1
ibn Daud, Abraham 31–2
ibn 'Ezra, Abraham 36–7
ibn 'Ezra, Moses 34
ibn Falaquera, Shem Tov ben Joseph 109, 112
ibn Gabirol, Solomon 34, 39–40
ibn Ghiyath, Isaac 43–5
ibn Jabir, Joseph 36, 87–8
ibn Janah, Jonah 33–4
ibn Jumay', Hibbat Allah 82–3
ibn Kaspi, Joseph 109
Ibn Masarrah 39–40
Ibn Maymun Synagogue 1
ibn Migash, Joseph ben Meir, ha-Levi 7–8, 43–5
ibn Rushd 40–1, 51, 56–8, 82–3, 113–14
ibn Sana' l-Mulk, Abu l-Qasim 19
Ibn Sina (Avicenna) 36–7, 40–1, 67–8, 83
ibn Tibbon, Samuel 23, 40–1, 80–1, 107–10
ibn Tumart, Muhammad 42–3
Immanuel ben Solomon 109
Immanuel of Rome 54–5
Iraq 43
Islam
Almohad 8–10, 42–3, 48–9
Almohad Creed (*al-'Aqida*) 41–3
Almoravids 7–10, 42–3
coerced conversions to 8–13, 89–90
disciplinary mastery 3
as imitative religion 91
Jewish community and 18–19, 29–30
Maimonides influence 19–20
Maimonides on 104–5
Maliki 13, 46–9
monotheism and 104–5
on rabbinic tradition 97
rational theology 38–9

religious common ground 103–4
Shi'i 101
Sufi 69–70
Sunni 17–18, 39, 42–3
taqiyya 8–10
Islamic civilization
Almohad Fez 11
Greek science and philosophy
37–8
Jewish culture in 6, 13, 17–19,
29–32, 34, 37–9, 91
literary Arabic in 29–32, 37–8
Neoplatonism 39–40
search for enlightenment 38
translation movement 37–8
Islamic East
al-Harizi in 25–6
Arabization of Jewish life 30
divine attributes 67–8
Jewish scholars 32–3, 37–8, 43–4
Muslim philosophers 36–7
rabbinical academies 43
Islamic law 8–10, 13, 19–20, 43–4
Islamic Spain *see* al-Andalus
Islamic West
Jewish community in 8–10
Maimonides' family in
13–15, 18–20
Maliki law 13
Talmudic scholarship 43
Isma'ilis 40
Israel and Israelites
chosen-ness 99–102
cultic animal sacrifice 71–3, 98
divine election of 98–101
escape to 13–15
Hebrew language and 58–9
influence of Maimonides 1
prophets of 52–3
religious development 71–3
Revelation at Mt. Sinai 58–9, 97
rivalries of 91
Tabernacle 73
Israeli, Isaac ben Solomon
39–40

Jacob ben Nathanel Fayyumi
89–90
Japheth ben Elijah 20–1
Jerusalem 13–15, 24
Jerusalem Temple 45–6, 73
Jesus 103–5
Jewish culture
Arabization of 29–34
Golden Age of 6–7, 30
influence of Maimonides 1–3,
106–7, 110–13
in Islamdom 6, 13, 17–19, 29–32,
34, 37–9, 91
Jewish law (*halakha*)
divine origin of 46–7
ethical behavior and 66–7
halakhic monographs 43–5
Hebrew language and 54–6
human perfection and 77
Judeo-Arabic biblical
exegesis 32–3
Maimonides on 3, 8–10, 15–16,
20–1, 43
philosophical principles 13,
56–60, 63–4, 93–4
pseudo-Muslims and 11–12
rabbinic Judaism 39
responsa (legal opinions)
22–3, 43–4
scientific inquiry in 56–8, 63–4
Sephardi 7–8
Talmud and 20–1, 92–3
Jewish religious scholars
anti-philosophical 110–13
biblical exegesis 35
Geonim 43
influence of Maimonides 108–10,
112–13
Islamic learning and 30
Judeo-Arabic tradition 31–4
Maimonidean Controversy
110–13
Maimonides works and 108–9

Index

137

Jewish religious scholars (*Continued*)
  Neoplatonism 39–40
  rabbinic law 30–1, 39, 46–7
  rationalist/anti-rationalist
    struggle 110–12
  rational theology 30, 32–3, 38–9
  revival of Hebrew 32–4, 58–9
  Sephardi Jewish identity 28–31
  Talmudic scholarship 43–4, 53
  Torah scholarship 46–7
  use of Arabic 29–31
  work in secrecy 12–13
Jews and Judaism
  Ashkenazi 1–2, 54–5, 109
  Babylonian rabbinic rites 18–19
  chosen-ness 99–102
  coerced conversions 8–13,
    19–20, 89–90
  divine law and 91, 101
  eschatological concepts 53
  Karaites 18–19
  persecution 8–12, 89–92
  principles for enlightened life
    48–9, 51–6, 92–3
  Rabbanites 18–19
  religious common ground 103–4
  sacred rituals 45–6
  tripartite community 18–19
  Yemenite 30–1, 85, 89–92, 107
Jonah ben Abraham Gerondi 112
Jonathan ben David ha-Cohen
  24–5, 35–6, 81–2
Joseph ben Judah ibn Simon
  as Maimonides disciple 19–20,
    23–4, 46, 56–7, 85
  on *Mishneh Torah* criticism 93
  as physician 8–10, 82–3
  *Silencing Epistle Concerning the
    Resurrection of the Dead* 93–4
Judah Halevi 34, 36–7, 39–40, 101–2
Judeo-Arabic education
  in Andalusia 30–4
  biblical Hebrew 30, 32–5
  halakhic monographs 43–4
  Hebrew poetry 34–5

K

Kaddish 107
Kairouan 30, 44–5
kalam (rational theology) 38–40
Karaites 18–19, 33–4, 38, 97
Kellner, Menachem 113
al-Kindi 39–40
Kitab al-durar (*The Book of Pearls:
  In Praise of Communities*)
  (al-Harizi) 25–6
Krochmal, Nahman 112–13

L

Latent Secret (Gorlitzki) 113–14
Letter of Consolation (Maimon)
  11–12
Levant 13–15, 17–18, 56, 93–4
Levi ben Gerson (Gersonides)
  108–9
Lucena 44–5
Lunel 24–5, 35–6, 81–2, 85

M

Maghrib
  ignorance of Torah 56
  Islamic learning in 11
  Jewish community in 4,
    11–12, 56
  persecution of Jews
    12–13, 89–90
Maimon, Solomon 109
Maimon ben Joseph 7–8,
  10–11, 15, 43
Maimonides, Abraham
  al-Harizi tribute to 108
  father's affection for 16–17, 23–4
  guardian of father's legacy
    17–20, 25–6, 82–3, 107, 111–12
  on opposition to *Guide* 110–12
  Wars of the Lord 111–12
Maimonides, David 10, 20–1,
  79–80

138

Maimonides, Moses 8–10*f*, 113–14*f*
  on Abraham and monotheism
    98–100, 102–3
  Almohad thought 41–3, 56
  Andalusi influences 28–32
  Aristotle and 1, 36–7, 40–3, 50,
    56–8, 61, 66–7
  biblical exegesis 34–5
  composition in Arabic 10, 21–2,
    28, 30–1, 36
  conflict with Karaites 18–19
  contemporary interpretations
    61–3
  contradictory positions 2,
    62–3, 79
  controversy and 17–19, 110–13
  as crypto-Jew 19–20, 41–2
  death of brother David 20–2,
    79–80
  on divine attributes 50–68,
    109–10
  on divine chosen-ness 99–102
  on divine commandments 13–15,
    54–5, 60–1, 71–3, 91
  on God's oneness 35, 40–2,
    52–3, 59–61, 66–7
  as Head of the Jews 17–20
  Hebrew language and 33–7
  humanity of 15–17, 87–90
  influence of 106–10, 112–15
  instruction by father 7–8, 10
  intellectual regimen 1–5, 12
  on Jewish law 8–10, 13–16, 21–3,
    48–9, 101–2
  on literal biblical interpretations
    35, 64–7
  mastery of the Torah 1–4, 12–13,
    20–1, 48–9
  messianic tradition 91–2, 105
  Muslim elite and 19–20
  Neoplatonism and 35–6, 40–1
  philosophical and scientific
    perspective 4–5, 12–13, 15,
    23–4, 28–9, 31, 40–1, 48–9,
    51–2, 56–8, 62–4, 70–1, 82–3

as physician 19–21, 23–4,
    82–3, 85, 113
  on prophecy 68–70
  reason-based theology 41–2,
    50–1, 56–7, 71
  religious and professional
    duties 79–82
  religious humanism 15–16, 85–7,
    95–9, 103–4
  repudiation of idolatry 22, 52–4,
    56–7, 73
  search for enlightenment 5,
    31–2, 51–3, 92–3
  Sephardi Jewish identity 28–31
  on solitude 78–81
  universalism 97–9, 102–3
  variations of name 1
  on World to Come 52–4, 58,
    64, 93–5
Maimonides, Moses. *Book of the
    Commandments*
  divine commandments in 13–15,
    54–5, 60–1, 70–3*f*
  on ethical behavior 74
  Jewish law in 21–2, 47–8
  linguistic virtue of 36
Maimonides, Moses. *Commentary
    on the Mishnah*
  divine reward and punishment 94
  doctrine of the messiah 99
  on ethical behavior 66–7
  fundamental principles in
    54–7, 66–7
  on human perfection 51,
    69–71, 74
  Jewish religious law in 13–15,
    21–2, 42–3, 47–8, 51, 97
  Judeo-Arabic language 30–1
  philosophical thought 48–9
  prophecy in 68–9
  revisions on God's eternality 61–2
  Sephardi Jewish identity in 28
  therapeutic method in 4
  translation to Hebrew 25–6
  on world to come 53–4

Maimonides, Moses. *Commentary on the Mishnah Avot* 50-1, 66-7, 74

Maimonides, Moses. *Commentary on the Mishnah* (*Pereq Heleq*)
fundamental principles in 54-5, 64
introduction 54
prophecy in 69-70
Sanhedrin 10 52-3
on world to come 52-3

Maimonides, Moses. Correspondence
on burden of daily routine 24, 80-2
Cairo Geniza 2, 8-10, 16-17
on crypto-Jews 11-12
humanity in 15-17, 87-90
with Ibn Rushd 113-14
with Jonathan ha-Kohen 24-5, 81-2
with Joseph ben Judah 19-20, 46, 93-4
on loss of brother David 79-80
ornate rhymed Hebrew prose 35-6
with rabbis of Provence 22-3, 93
responsa (legal opinions) 22-3, 30-1, 43, 85-8, 96, 106*f*
Yemeni Jews 15-16

Maimonides, Moses. *Epistle to Yemen*
Andalusi identity 28
correspondence with Jewish community 22-3, 30-1, 89-92, 96, 103-4
prophecy in 68
religious humanism in 15-16, 91-2

Maimonides, Moses. *Guide for the Perplexed*
Andalusi learning in 28-9
contradictions in 62-3
creation narrative in 98
criticism of 93, 110-12

dedication to Joseph ben Judah 19-20, 23
directive to love God 58-9
on divine attributes 67-8
divine reward and punishment 94
on divine unity 66-7
enlightenment of 51-2
on ethical behavior 74
fundamental principles in 56-7, 66-7
God's existence in 64-5
on God's image 97-8
Hebrew Bible in 34-5
on human perfection 74-7, 79, 103
Jewish commentaries on 109
Judeo-Arabic language 30-1
prophecy in 68-70
Provencal followers 24-6
rationality in 23, 50, 71
on religious common ground 103-4
on resurrection 61-2
scriptural based sermons 109
on solitude 78-9
translation to Hebrew 25-6, 40-1, 107-10
translation to Latin 109-10

Maimonides, Moses. *Mishneh Torah* (The Code of Jewish Law)
Book of Agriculture 103
Book of Judges 99, 105
Book of Knowledge 30-1, 54-60, 63-4, 110-11
codification of Jewish law 10, 13, 21-3, 45-9, 103-4
composition of 56
creation narrative in 98
criticism of 92-4
directive to love God 57-61
divine reward and punishment 94
doctrine in 22, 42-3, 55-6

fundamental principles in
56–60, 66–7, 97–8
on God's image 103
on God's oneness 60–1
on Islam 104
Jewish scholars and 108–9
knowledge of God 57–61
medicine in 84–5
medieval manuscript 46–7f
messianic age 105
Oral Law in 97
prophecy in 68
rabbinic Hebrew language
31, 35–6
religious humanism 85–7
religious restoration and reform
45–6
universalism 103
Maimonides, Moses. *Treatise on
Resurrection*
defense of views on
resurrection 22–3, 30–1, 61–2,
68, 94–5
direction to world to come 95
influence of 96
translation to Hebrew 25–6
Maimonides, Moses. Writings of
On Asthma 83
Book of Knowledge 84–5
On the Causes of Symptoms 83
On Coitus 23–4, 83
*Commentary on Hippocrates'
Aphorisms* 83
*Compendia from the Works
of Galen* 83
consilia 23–4
Eight Chapters 4, 68, 74, 84–5
*On the Elucidation of Some
Symptoms and the Response
to Them* 23–4
Epistle on Apostasy 11–12
Epistle on Forced Conversion 4
Epistle on Martyrdom
4, 89–90
Glossary of Drug Names 83

Glossary on Pharmaceuticals
28–9
Guide of the Perplexed 23
On Hemorrhoids 83
Letter on Astrology 22–3,
28, 50–1
Letter to Hasdai Halevi 22–3
Letter to Joseph ben Judah
19–20, 22–3
Letter to Joseph ibn Jabir 22–3
*Letter to Obadiah the
Proselyte* 22–3
Letter to the Sages of Lunel 22–3
Medical Aphorisms 33–4, 83
"Parable of the Palace," 74–6
On Poisons 83
On the Regimen of Health 23–4,
82–3f
Thirteen Principles of Faith
54–5, 112
*Treatise on Lunar
Intercalation* 10
Treatise on the Art of Logic 10,
31, 50, 79. See also
specific works
*Maimonides and Spinoza Come
to Dinner* (Bejarano
Gutierrez) 113–14
Maliki 13, 46–9
al-Ma'mun 37–8
medicine
ethical behavior and 84
in Islamdom 37–8
Maimonides on 4
Maimonides practice of 12–13,
19–21, 23–4, 82–5, 113
Maimonides writings on 23–4,
28–9, 82–5f
in *Mishneh Torah* 84–5
religious significance of 83–5
Menahem ha-Me'iri 109
Mendelsohn, Moses 112–13
Messiah 24–5, 91–2, 99–101
Metaphysics (Aristotle) 41–2
Mishnaic Tractate Sanhedrin 52–3

monotheism
  Abraham and 98, 102–3
  Christianity and 105
  idolatry and 97–8
  Islam and 88, 104–5
  in *Mishneh Torah* 103–5
Morocco 1, 8–13. *See also*
    Fez, Morocco
Moses (biblical)
  comparisons to 1, 24–5
  human perfection and 76
  humility 15–16
  prophecy 68–70, 90–1, 101–2
  Revelation at Mt. Sinai 58–9, 97
  Torah foundations 46–7,
    52–3, 61
Moses ben Hanokh 43
Moses ben Solomon 109
Moses Narboni 109
Muhammad 41–3, 69–70, 105
Muslims *see* Islam
mutakallimun 38–40
Mu'tazila 38–9

N

Nahmanides (Moses ben Nahman)
    107, 110–11
Neoplatonism 35–6, 39–41
Nimoy, Leonard 113–14
Nissim ben Jacob ibn Shahin 44–5

O

Obadiah the Proselyte 87–8

P

Palestine 13–15, 18–19, 43
philosophy
  Almohad 41–3
  Andalusi 28–9, 31–2
  Aristotelian 1, 31–2, 38–43,
    56–7, 61, 74, 84–5
  Greek 37–8

Hebrew Bible 32–3, 54
Jewish law and 13, 56–60, 63–4
Maimonidean Controversy 110–11
of Maimonides 38–43, 50–1
Maimonides education in 10,
    12–13, 15
Muslim 36–40
Neoplatonic 35–6, 39–41
physicians and 82–3
reason-based 30, 40–1
relationship with Torah 13,
    23–4, 42–3, 62–3
religious attacks on 61–2
revelation and religious 51
Plotinus 67–8
prophecy 68–70, 90–1
Provence
  Hebrew translation of *Guide*
    23, 25–6
  influence of Maimonides 15–16
  Jewish community in 15–16,
    22–3, 25–6, 108
  Maimonidean Controversy
    110–12
Ptolemy 28–9
Putnam, Brenda 114*f*

Q

al-Qadi al-Fadil 19–20
Qimhi, David 112
Qur'an
  Almohad Creed (*al-'Aqida*) 41–2
  Arabic language 36–7
  coerced conversions 8–10
  Hebrew aesthetics 32–3
  Isma'ili exegesis 40
  Muslim exegesis 30, 32–4, 40

R

Rabbanites 18–19, 32–3,
    38–9, 46–7
Rambam: The Story of Maimonides
    (film) 113–14

142

Rambam: The Story of Maimonides (graphic novel) 113–14
Rasa'il ikhwan al-safa' (*Epistles of the Pure Brethren*) 39–40
religious humanism 8–10, 15–16, 85–7, 97–8
resurrection
  in *The Guide* 61–2
  Maimonides on 22–4, 30–1, 53, 61–2, 92–5
  in *Mishneh Torah* 61–2
  rabbinic doctrine 30–1, 53, 92–5

S

Sa'adia Gaon
  biblical Hebrew 32–7, 39–40
  Book of Beliefs and Opinions 39
  on divine attributes 67–8
  halakhic monographs 43–4
  Quranic exegesis 32–4
  rational theology 39
  responsa (legal opinions) 43–4
  Talmudic scholarship 43–4
Saladin 17–20, 23–4, 89–90
Samuel ben 'Eli 22–3, 93–5
Samuel ben Hofni Gaon 32–3, 43–4
Samuel the Nagid 34
Schechter, Solomon 113–14
sciences
  Greek 31–2, 37–8
  in Islamdom 37–40
  Jewish law and 56–8, 63–4
  Judeo-Arabic biblical exegesis 32–3
  Maimonidean Controversy 110–11
  Maimonides study and teaching 12–13, 15
  physicians and 82–3
  Torah study and 23–4, 53–4, 57–8
Sephardi Jews
  halakhic tradition 7–8

heroic folktales on Maimonides 107
influence on Maimonides 43
introduction to *Pereq Heleq* 54–5
Maimonides as 1, 7–8, 28–9
al-Sijilmasi, Solomon ben Judah 8–10
solitude 78–81
Solomon ben Abraham 110–12
Spain 1, 6, 8–10, 22, 30. *See also* al-Andalus; Iberia
Spinoza, Baruch (Benedict) 112–13
Sufficient Guide, The (Tanhum ben Joseph) 108–9

T

Tahkemoni (al-Harizi) 25–6
Talmud
  Babylonian 18–19, 51–2
  chosen-ness 99–100
  halakhic monographs 43–5
  Jewish law 20–1, 92–3
  Judeo-Arabic education 31–2
  Maimonides on 20–2
  rabbinic tradition and 51–3
  scholarship 43–4, 92–3
Tanhum ben Joseph ha-Yerushalmi 108–9
taqiyya 8–10
Themistius 40–1
Thomas Aquinas 109–10
Torah
  chosen-ness 100–1
  divine attributes 50–67
  divine origin of 46–7, 52–3
  epistemological foundations 46–7
  fundamental principles of 56–8
  Hebrew language and 54–6
  Jewish understanding of 55–6
  legal interpretations 35
  Maimonides mastery of 1–4, 20–1, 48–9, 51–2
  oral 1–2, 6, 31, 46–7, 68, 93

Torah (*Continued*)
  philosophical perspective 5, 23–4, 42–3, 57–8, 62–3, 108
  rationality of commandments 70–1
  resurrection in 95
  scientific inquiry and 23–4, 53–4, 57–8
  written 21–2, 46–7, 93, 95
Twersky, Isadore 36, 79–80

U

Umayyad Andalusi emirate 6

Y

Yemen
  ignorance of Torah 56, 85, 91–2
  Jewish community in 93–4, 107
  Judeo-Arabic commentary on *Pereq Heleq* 54–5
  persecution of Jews 15–16, 30–1, 85, 89–92
  rabbinic leaders 91–2

Z

Zaydi Shi'a 15–16, 89–90
Zoroastrians 29–30

PHILOSOPHY OF RELIGION
A Very Short Introduction
Tim Bayne

What is the philosophy of religion? How can we distinguish it from theology on the one hand and the psychology/sociology of religious belief on the other? What does it mean to describe God as 'eternal'? And should religious people want there to be good arguments for the existence of God, or is religious belief only authentic in the absence of these good arguments?

In this *Very Short Introduction* Tim Bayne introduces the field of philosophy of religion, and engages with some of the most burning questions that philosophers discuss. Considering how 'religion' should be defined, and whether we even need to be able to define it in order to engage in the philosophy of religion, he goes on to discuss whether the existence of God matters. Exploring the problem of evil, Bayne also debates the connection between faith and reason, and the related question of what role reason should play in religious contexts. Shedding light on the relationship between science and religion, Bayne finishes by considering the topics of reincarnation and the afterlife.

www.oup.com/vsi

ISLAMIC HISTORY
A Very Short Introduction
Adam J. Silverstein

Does history matter? This book argues not that history matters, but that Islamic history does. This *Very Short Introduction* introduces the story of Islamic history; the controversies surrounding its study; and the significance that it holds - for Muslims and for non-Muslims alike. Opening with a lucid overview of the rise and spread of Islam, from the seventh to twenty first century, the book charts the evolution of what was originally a small, localised community of believers into an international religion with over a billion adherents. Chapters are also dedicated to the peoples - Arabs, Persians, and Turks - who shaped Islamic history, and to three representative institutions - the mosque, jihad, and the caliphate - that highlight Islam's diversity over time.

'The book is extremely lucid, readable, sensibly organised, and wears its considerable learning, as they say, 'lightly'.'

BBC History Magazine

www.oup.com/vsi